Fire and Res Service Manual

Volume 2
Fire Service Operations

Safe Work at Height

London: TSO

Published by TSO (The Stationery Office) and available from:

Online
www.tsoshop.co.uk

Mail, Telephone, Fax & E-mail
TSO
PO Box 29, Norwich, NR3 1GN
Telephone orders/General enquiries: 0870 600 5522
Fax orders: 0870 600 5533
E-mail: customer.services@tso.co.uk
Textphone 0870 240 3701

TSO Shops
123 Kingsway, London, WC2B 6PQ
020 7242 6393 Fax 020 7242 6394
16 Arthur Street, Belfast BT1 4GD
028 9023 8451 Fax 028 9023 5401
71 Lothian Road, Edinburgh EH3 9AZ
0870 606 5566 Fax 0870 606 5588

TSO@Blackwell and other Accredited Agents

Published with the permission of the Department for Communities and Local Government on behalf of the Controller of Her Majesty's Stationery Office

ISBN (10) 0 11 341312 2
ISBN (13) 978 0 11 341312 6

Cover photographs: Chris Hawkins; The National Rope Users Group; Hampshire Fire and Rescue Service
Part-title page photograph: Chris Hawkins

Printed in Great Britain on material containing 75% post-consumer waste and 25% ECF pulp.

Printed in the United Kingdom for The Stationery Office
ID545954C 11/06 C25

Safe Work at Height

Contents

Purpose of this Guidance		vii
Scope		vii
Acknowledgments		viii

Chapter 1 – Strategic Framework — 1

The Legal Framework — 1

1.1 Introduction — 1

1.2 European Legislation — 1

1.3 United Kingdom Legislation — 1
- 1.3.1 The Health and Safety at Work Etc. Act 1974 — 1
- 1.3.2 Management of Health and Safety at Work Regulations 1999 — 2
- 1.3.3 Work at Height Regulations 2005 (WAHR) — 3
- 1.3.4 Confined Spaces Regulations 1997 — 7
- 1.3.5 Personal Protective Equipment at Work Regulations 1992 and Personal Protective Equipment Regulations 2002 (PEP) — 7
- 1.3.6 The Provision and Use of Work Equipment Regulations 1998 (PUWER) — 7
- 1.3.7 Lifting Operations and Lifting Equipment Regulations 1998 (LOLER) — 7

1.4 Organisational Roles and Responsibilities — 8
- 1.4.1 Fire and Rescue Authorities — 8
- 1.4.2 Principal Officers/Brigade Managers — 8
- 1.4.3 Management of Work at Height Activities — 8

1.5 Key Hazards and Risks — 9
- 1.5.1 Equipment — 9
- 1.5.2 Nature of the Work — 10
- 1.5.3 Work Site and Prevailing Environmental Conditions — 11
- 1.5.4 Equipment Use — 12

1.6 Developing Safe Systems of Work — 12
- 1.6.1 Clothing — 12
- 1.6.2 Before Work at Height — 12
- 1.6.3 During Work at Height — 14
- 1.6.4 Post Work at Height — 17

Chapter 2 – Operational Practices — 19

2.1 General Techniques — 19
- 2.1.1 Collective Safeguards for Arresting Falls — 19
- 2.1.2 Individual Protection — 20

2.2 Access Techniques — 27
- 2.2.1 Working Platforms (General) — 27
- 2.2.2 Scaffolding and Access Towers — 27

2.2.3	Mobile Elevated Work Platforms (MEWPs)	28
2.2.4	Continuity of Means of Protection	29
2.2.5	Portable Ladders	29
2.2.6	Fixed Ladders	30
2.2.7	Ropes, Harnesses and Associated Equipment	31

2.3 Systems of Work — 38
| 2.3.1 | Anchors and Anchor Systems | 38 |

2.4 Securing Casualties, Equipment and Other Items — 46
2.4.1	Knots	46
2.4.2	Lifting, Lowering and Hauling	51
2.4.3	Winches and Pulley Systems	54
2.4.4	Mechanical Advantage and Velocity Ratio	55
2.4.5	Securing Casualties and Performing Rescues from Height	59
2.4.6	Casualty Management	61

2.5 Operational Environments — 62
2.5.1	Existing Places of Work	62
2.5.2	Unprotected Edges	62
2.5.3	Roofs – Flat Roofs, Sloping Roofs and Fragile Roofs	64
2.5.4	Flat Roofs	64
2.5.5	Sloping Roofs	64
2.5.6	Fragile Roofs/Surfaces	65
2.5.7	FRS Vehicles	67
2.5.8	Service and Utility Structures	68
2.5.9	Trees	69
2.5.10	Collapsed Structures	69
2.5.11	Working Near Water	69
2.5.12	Confined Spaces	70

Chapter 3 – Equipment — 71

3.1 Selection of Equipment — 71
3.2 Ladders and Aerial Appliances — 71
3.2.1	Portable Ladders For Fire Service Use	71
3.2.2	Turntable Ladders (TL)	72
3.2.3	Hydraulic Platforms (HP)	72
3.2.4	Aerial Ladder Platforms (ALP)	74

3.3 Working Platforms — 74

3.4 Textile Based Equipment — 75
3.4.1	General	75
3.4.2	Webbing Slings	75
3.4.3	Lanyards	75
3.4.4	Safety and Work Harnesses	76

3.5 Metal-Based Equipment — 76
3.5.1	General	76
3.5.2	Connectors (karabiners, safety hooks, screw links)	77
3.5.3	Pulleys	77
3.5.4	Wire Strops	78
3.5.5	General Metal Hardware	78
3.5.6	Rope Control Devices	78

	3.5.7	Tripods/Quadpods/Frames	79
	3.5.8	Stretchers	80
3.6	Ropes		80
	3.6.1	General	80
	3.6.2	Categories of Rope	84
	3.6.3	Associated Rope Working Equipment	85
3.7	Equipment Identification		85
3.8	Stowage of Ropes and Associated Equipment		86
3.9	Equipment Inspections, Examinations and Tests		86
	3.9.1	Pre-use and after-use checks	86
	3.9.2	Detailed Inspection	86
	3.9.3	Maintenance	87
	3.9.4	Record Keeping	87
	3.9.5	Disposal of Equipment	88

Chapter 4 – Training — 89

4.1	General Requirements		89
	4.1.1	Training Structure	89
	4.1.2	Instructors	89
4.2	Training Requirements for all Firefighters		90
4.3	Specialist Rope Operator Support Duties		92
4.4	Specialist Rope Operator Duties		94
4.5	Rope Work Supervisor		96
4.6	Rope Work Instructor		97
4.7	Technical Rope Work Officer		98
4.8	Continuation Training and CPD		98
4.9	Use of Live Casualties		99

Bibliography — 101

Glossary — 103

Appendix 'A' – Work at Height Flow Chart — 110

Safe Work at Height

Purpose of this Guidance

The Work at Height Regulations 2005 (WAHR) are made under the Health and Safety at Work etc. Act 1974 (HSW Act) and bring into effect the requirements of Council Directive 2001/45/EC that amended the Use of Work Equipment Directive (89/655/EC). This amendment is known as the 'Temporary Work at Height Directive'. The primary objective of WAHR is to ensure that all work at height is performed safely. These Regulations apply to all workplaces where the HSW Act applies.

This document gives guidance on legislation relevant to work at height and identifies good practice, which supports safe systems of work. The guidance is for use by fire and rescue services for planning operational service delivery and training.

Scope

Work at height covers all work activities where there is a possibility that a fall likely to result in personal injury could occur. Work at Height specifically includes access to and exit from a place of work. Examples of work at height include:

- All training or work where there is a risk of falling.
- Using a ladder.
- Working on an aerial appliance decking or platform.
- Working on the roof of a vehicle.
- Rope rescue work and training.
- Working in confined spaces.
- Working on cliffs.
- Tower crane rescues.
- Fire fighting and rescues on embankments, docks and quays.

- Offshore fire fighting and rescue.
- Climbing fixed structures.
- Working close to an excavation area where someone could fall.
- Working near a fragile surface.
- Vehicle and property maintenance.

The following are not considered to be work at height, but they would need to be covered by risk assessments if they posed a significant risk.

- Slips and trips on the level.
- Falls on permanent stairs if there is no structural work or maintenance being undertaken.
- Work on the upper floors of a building where there is no risk from falling.

Acknowledgments

The contribution of the following individuals and organisations to the production of this manual is acknowledged:

Diane Bell	Her Majesty's Fire Service Inspectorate
Chris Bilby	Leicestershire Fire and Rescue Service
Lawrie Booth	Cambridgeshire Fire and Rescue Service
John Burke	Cleveland Fire Brigade
Phil Crook	Hampshire Fire and Rescue Service
Roy Harold	Buckinghamshire Fire and Rescue Service
Gary Jeffery	Essex County Fire and Rescue Service
Steve Jones	South Wales Fire and Rescue Service
Denys Rama	Her Majesty's Fire Service Inspectorate
Mark Wilson	Essex County Fire and Rescue Service

Chief Fire Officers' Association
Fire and Rescue Service National Rope Users' Group
Health and Safety Executive

Safe Work at Height

Chapter 1 – Strategic Framework

THE LEGAL FRAMEWORK

1.1 Introduction

This chapter attempts to provide an overview of the legal framework which fire and rescue services (FRS) have to operate within. It gives an insight into the legislative requirements, both from the UK and from the EU, in the form of EU Directives, which govern UK health and safety law.

1.2 European Legislation

The Single European Act of 1987 amended the Treaty of Rome permitting the Community to introduce minimum standards for the health and safety of workers. The means of standard setting is by Directives; these bind each member state but leave to each the means of implementing Directives into its own law.

The Framework Directive is the first and most important of the post-1987 Directives and was incorporated in to UK law through the Management of Health and Safety at Work Regulations 1992. Employers are required to:

- Avoid risks to safety and health.
- Evaluate risks which cannot be avoided,
- Combat risks at source, adapting the work to the individual.
- Adapt to technical progress.
- Replace the dangerous by the non-dangerous or the less dangerous.
- Develop a coherent overall prevention policy.
- Give collective protective measures priority over individual measures.
- Give appropriate instructions to workers.

1.3 United Kingdom Legislation

1.3.1 The Health and Safety at Work etc. Act 1974

General duties of employers to their employees

(1) It shall be the duty of every employer to ensure, so far as is reasonably practicable, the health, safety and welfare at work of all his employees.

(2) Without prejudice to the generality of an employer's duty under the preceding subsection, the matters to which that duty extends include in particular –

(a) the provision and maintenance of plant and systems of work that are, so far as is reasonably practicable, safe and without risks to health;

(b) arrangements for ensuring, so far as is reasonably practicable, safety and absence of risks to health in connection with the use, handling, storage and transport of articles and substances;

(c) the provision of such information, instruction, training and supervision as is necessary to ensure, so far as is reasonably practicable, the health and safety at work of his employees;

(d) so far as is reasonably practicable as regards any place of work under the employer's control, the maintenance of it in a condition that is safe and without risks to health and the provision and maintenance of means of access to and egress from it that are safe and without such risks;

(e) the provision and maintenance of a working environment for his employees that is, so far as is reasonably practicable, safe, without risks to health, and adequate as regards facilities and arrangements for their welfare at work.

Note: *Pope v Gould (H M Inspector of Health and Safety) (20 June 1996, unreported)* illustrates the stringent way in which the courts enforce this section. In this case, the employer argued that because he had instructed the employee to operate machinery in a particular way, and the employee had not followed his instructions, he was not liable. However, it was held that this section is not concerned solely with the giving of instructions; rather it imposes upon the employer positive duties in relation to ensuring safe systems of work and safe machinery. It is not sufficient for instructions of a health and safety nature merely to be given to employees; an employer must also ensure that those instructions are carried out.

General duties of employers and self-employed to persons other than their employees

Employers and the self employed are required to conduct their work activities to ensure, so far as is reasonably practicable, that people not in their employment are not exposed to risks to their health or safety.

General duties of employees at work

Employees must:

- Take reasonable care for their health and safety and that of other people who may be affected by their acts or omissions at work.

- Co-operate with their employer in health and safety matters.

- Not interfere with or misuse anything provided for their health and safety.

1.3.2 Management of Health and Safety at Work Regulations 1999

Regulation 3: Risk Assessment
This requires all employers and self-employed people to assess the risks to workers and any others who may be affected by their work or business. All employers should carry out a systematic general examination of their work activities, to identify the risks to health and safety to any person arising out of, or in connection with their work.

Where the assessment identifies significant risk, adequate control measures must be implemented, the process recorded, monitored and reviewed.

Regulation 4: Principles of prevention to be applied
The general hierarchy of control applies to all work at height.

- Avoid risks.
- Evaluate risks which cannot be avoided.
- Combat risks at source.
- Adapt work to the individual.
- Adapt to technical progress.
- Replace the dangerous by the non-dangerous or the less dangerous.
- Develop a coherent overall prevention policy.
- Give collective protective measures priority over individual protective measures.
- Give appropriate instructions to employees.

Regulation 8: Procedures for serious and imminent danger and for danger areas
When undertaking training or rescue operations at height, suitable and sufficient emergency plans should be factored into generic risk assessments and procedures. This requirement is within both the Management Regulations and the Work at Height Regulations.

Regulation 11: Co-operation and co-ordination
When staff from more than one employer are in the workplace (including the incident ground) co-ordination and co-operation is required to ensure that safety arrangements adopted are adequate.

Regulation 13: Capabilities and training
When allocating work to employees, FRS's should

ensure that the demands of the job do not exceed the employees' ability to carry out the work without risk to themselves or others.

Regulation 14: Employees' duties
Employees have a duty to co-operate with their employer to enable the employer to comply with statutory duties for health and safety. Employees should also notify any shortcomings in the health and safety arrangements, even when no immediate danger exists, so that employers can take remedial action if needed.

Regulation 16: Risk assessment in respect of new or expectant mothers
Risk assessments for work at height should take account of women who may be new or expectant mothers and identify the preventive and protective measures that are required in Regulation 3.

1.3.3 Work At Height Regulations 2005 (WAHR)

Regulation 1 Citation and commencement
The WAHR came into force on 6th April 2005.

Regulation 2 Interpretation
This regulation defines a number of key issues including work at height, personal fall protection systems, fragile surfaces and working platforms.

Regulation 3 Application
This regulation sets out that the WAHR apply in Great Britain to employers and the self employed; it exempts certain dockside, offshore and ship board activities.

Regulation 4: Organisation and planning
This regulation states that WAH should be planned, supervised and carried out in a manner which is, so far as is reasonably practicable, safe. Planning for emergencies is included. WAH should only be carried out when the weather conditions do not jeopardise the health or safety of those involved in the work. Emergency services acting in an emergency are exempt from this restriction.

The exemption in Regulation 4(4) for emergency services acting in an emergency is to enable the work of the emergency services during the emergency or rescue phase to proceed. The HSE enforcement operational circular advises their inspectors that:

"Regulation 4 duties should not hinder the work of the emergency services while they are working in the emergency rescue phase when life may be in danger or life saving is being attempted. The intention is not to hinder the speed or effectiveness of emergency services acting in this emergency phase but when this phase has passed, the Regulations will be expected to apply as normal. Emergency services will be expected to have generic training and experience available to deal with risks associated with the emergency phase. They should also be able to use dynamic risk assessments to cope with changing circumstances."

Regulation 5 Competence
This regulation requires that all those involved in WAH should be competent, or if being trained, be properly supervised by a competent person.

For the purposes of this fire and rescue service guidance, a competent person is one who understands their responsibilities under these Regulations and can demonstrate that they have sufficient professional or technical training, knowledge, actual experience, and authority[1] to enable them to:

- Carry out their assigned duties at the level of responsibility allocated to them.
- Understand any potential hazards related to the work (or equipment) under consideration.
- Detect any technical defects or omissions in that work (or equipment), recognise any implications for health and safety caused by those defects or omissions and be able to specify remedial actions to mitigate those implications.

Regulation 6 Avoidance of risks from work at height
This regulation sets out the hierarchy of control measures for performing WAH, based on the employers risk assessment under the Management

---

1 Note: "authority" here means delegated authority to the individual by his employer to carry out a certain function or duty.

of Health and Safety at Work Regulations. The hierarchy is

AVOID WAH if you can.

If this is not possible then take suitable and sufficient steps to

PREVENT the risk of a fall, including
- Selection of an existing work place that does not require additional measures to prevent a fall and where this is not possible
- Selection of the most suitable work equipment to prevent a fall occurring

MINIMISE the distance and consequences of any fall.

When selecting work equipment, priority should be given to collective fall protection measures over personal protection.

Regulation 7 Selection of work equipment
This regulation sets out the general principles to be applied when selecting work equipment for WAH. These principles include, working conditions, distance and consequences of a fall, duration and frequency of use, emergency evacuation and additional risks present when the equipment is being set up or taken down.

Regulation 8 Requirements for particular work equipment
This regulation requires that work equipment selected for a particular task must comply with the requirements laid out in the appropriate schedules to the Regulations:

- Guard rails, toe boards, barrier or similar collective means (Schedule 2).
- Working platforms, including aerial appliances (Schedule 3. part 1).
- Collective Safeguards (Schedule 4).
- Personal fall protection systems (Schedule 5, part 1).
- Work restraint (Schedule 5, part 5).
- Work positioning (Schedule 5, parts 2 and 3).
- Fall arrest systems (Schedule 5, part 4).
- Ladders (Schedule 6).

Regulation 9 Fragile surfaces
This regulation sets out the requirements needed to prevent people falling through fragile surfaces. It says that no person at work should pass across, or work on or from, a fragile surface where it is reasonably practicable to carry out this work safely by some other means. Fragile surfaces must be indicated by warning notices, but fire and rescue services, acting in an emergency are exempt from this requirement.

Regulation 10 Falling objects
This regulation requires steps to be taken to prevent objects falling from height where injury could result. The risk of falling objects causing injury should be minimised by keeping strict control over the working area and that any materials or objects stored at height should be secured.

Regulation 11 Danger areas
This regulation requires any danger area where someone or something could fall and cause injury to be clearly indicated and actions taken to prevent people entering the danger area.

Regulation 12 Inspection of equipment
This regulation sets out the inspection and recording requirements for equipment provided for WAH. An inspection can vary from a simple visual check to a detailed comprehensive inspection, which may include some dismantling and testing.

Regulation 13 Inspection of places of Work at Height
This regulation states that the work surface and every parapet, permanent rail or other such fall protection measure of every place of work at height, so far as is reasonably practicable, is checked on each occasion before the place is used.

Regulation 14 Duties of persons at work
This regulation reflects the duties placed on employees by the Management of Health and Safety at Work Regulations and emphasises the importance, in the context of work at height, of employees using the equipment provided by the employer to prevent or mitigate falls from height and of doing so in accordance with training they have received and instructions concerning its use.

Regulation 15 – Exemption by the Health and Safety Executive
This specifies the nature and extent to which the

HSE can exempt people, activities, work equipment or premises from the requirements of the Regulations.

Regulation 16 Exemption of the armed forces
This regulation sets out a system for exemption of the armed forces in the interests of national security.

Regulation 17 Amendment of PUWER 1998
This regulations adds equipment to which regulation 12 (inspections) of the WAH Regulations applies to regulation 6(5) of the Provision and Use of Work Equipment Regulations 1998.

Regulation 18 Repeal of section 24 of the Factories Act 1961
This regulation repeals section 24 of the Factories Act 1961.

Regulation 19 Revocation of Instruments
This regulation sets out a number of consequential revocations to a number of regulations specified in column 1 of schedule 8 to the WAHR.

Schedule 1 – Requirements for places of work at height
This schedule sets out the requirements for existing places of work at height, including means of access and egress. Existing places of work at height are those that do not require any additional safety measures to prevent a fall from occurring; the requirements of this schedule include comment on:

- Strength and rigidity of the structure.
- Suitable dimensions to carry out the work and permit the safe passage of plant and equipment.
- Provision of suitable edge protection – the height of sills and parapets should be determined by a risk assessment under the Management Regulations, and activities in the area should be controlled by the findings of the risk assessment.
- Means to prevent objects from falling.
- Means to prevent slipping and tripping.

Schedule 2 Requirements for guardrails
This schedule sets out similar requirements to schedule 1 for work equipment such as aerial appliances and scaffold towers. The height of

guardrails and edge protection measures (e.g. for drill towers/aerial appliances) should be determined by risk assessment. For construction work, the schedule sets the minimum height for guard-rails to be at least 950 mm.

Schedule 3 Requirements for working platforms
This schedule is in two parts, the first part sets out the general requirements for:

- Working platforms, including Mobile Elevated Work Platforms (MEWPS). Fire and rescue service aerial appliances fitted with a cage fall within the definition of a MEWP.
- Scaffolding.
- Ground conditions, stability of the platform and supporting structures, working surfaces, construction and loading.

The second part of the schedule covers detailed requirements for scaffolding.

Schedule 4 Requirements for Collective Safeguards for Arresting Falls
This schedule sets out the requirements for collective safeguards to be suitably anchored, of sufficient strength and stability to withstand loading in the event of a fall and that in the event of a fall by any person the safeguard does not itself cause injury to that person.

Schedule 5 Requirements for Personal Fall Protection Systems
This schedule is in five parts,

Part 1 sets out the general requirements for all personal fall protection systems, including fall prevention, work restraint, work positioning, fall arrest, rescue systems, and rope access and positioning techniques. Before using such systems a risk assessment must indicate that:

- The work can so far as is reasonably practicable be performed safely while using that system and the use of other, safer work equipment is not reasonably practicable.
- The user and a sufficient number of available persons have received adequate training specific to the operations envisaged, including rescue procedures.

All personal fall protection equipment must:

- Be suitable and of sufficient strength for the purposes for which it is being used, having regard to the work being carried out and any foreseeable loading.
- Where necessary, fit the user and be correctly fitted.
- Be designed to minimise injury to the user and, where necessary, be adjusted to prevent the user falling or slipping from it, should a fall occur.
- Be so designed, installed and used as to prevent unplanned or uncontrolled movement of the user.

Part 2 sets out the additional requirements for work positioning systems, including the requirement:

- For a suitable backup system for preventing or arresting a fall.
- That where the system includes a line as a backup system, the user is connected to it.
- Where it is not reasonably practicable to provide a backup system, all practicable measures are taken to ensure that the work positioning system does not fail.

Part 3 sets out the additional requirements for rope access and positioning techniques, including that a rope access or positioning technique shall:

- Involve a system comprising at least two separately anchored lines, of which one ("the working line") is used as a means of access, egress and support and the other is the safety line.
- Ensure the user is provided with a suitable harness and is connected by it to the working line and the safety line.
- Ensure the working line is equipped with safe means of ascent and descent and has a self-locking system to prevent the user falling should he lose control of his movements and the safety line is equipped with a mobile fall protection system which is connected to and travels with the user of the system.
- Only use a single rope system where a risk assessment has demonstrated that the use of a second line would entail higher risk to persons and appropriate measures have been taken to ensure safety.

Part 4 sets out the additional requirements for fall arrest systems including the requirement for a suitable means of absorbing energy and limiting the forces applied to the user's body. A fall arrest system must not be used where:

- There is a risk of the line being cut.
- There is no clear zone beneath the work area and its safe use requires a clear zone. including allowing for any pendulum effect.
- Its performance would be compromised or rendered unsafe.

Part 5 sets out the additional requirements for work restraint systems to be used correctly and designed so that they prevent the user from getting into a position in which a fall can occur.

Schedule 6 Requirements for Ladders

This schedule requires employers to ensure that a ladder is used for work at height only if a risk assessment has demonstrated that the use of alternative work equipment is not justified by the circumstances, the short duration of use or existing features on site which can't be altered.

The surface on which a ladder is pitched must be stable, firm, of sufficient strength and suitable composition to support the ladder and any intended load. Portable ladders must be prevented from slipping during use by:

- Securing at or near their upper or lower ends. or
- Providing an effective anti-slip or other effective stability device. or
- Any other arrangement of equivalent effectiveness, which could include 'footing' the ladder and the use of support or handling poles in accordance with accepted fire and rescue service practices.

Ladders must protrude sufficiently above the place of landing unless other measures have been taken to ensure a firm handhold. Extension ladders must be resting securely on their pawls before use. When using ladders, a secure handhold and secure support must be available to the user, who must maintain a safe handhold when carrying a load.

Step ladders may be exempt from the requirement for a secure handhold when a load is carried, but only when a risk assessment identifies low risk and a short duration of use.

Schedule 7 Particulars to be included in a report of inspection

This schedule sets out the detail of the contents of an inspection report on equipment provided for WAH.

Schedule 8 Revocation of Instruments

This schedule provides details of statutory instruments revoked by the WAHR.

1.3.4 Confined Spaces Regulations 1997

The Confined Spaces Regulations, 1997 apply to all premises and work situations where a work area is a fully or partially enclosed space and a defined hazard is present. These regulations require employers to:

- Avoid entry to confined spaces.
- Where it is not possible to avoid entry, establish and follow a safe system of work.
- Ensure the safe system of work includes suitable and sufficient emergency arrangements.

Fire and rescue service operations in confined spaces will often involve work at height. In supplying equipment to account for the risks presented by work at height there is always a need to provide a suitable recovery system that ensures safe egress is maintained even if personnel are injured. Consideration should be given to ensuring the compatibility of the equipment and systems of work to meet these requirements.

1.3.5 Personal Protective Equipment at Work Regulations 1992 and Personal Protective Equipment Regulations 2002 (PPE)

Some items of equipment that are not normally designated as PPE could become so when assembled into a work system for work at height. Examples may include ropes, harnesses and associated equipment which are assembled into a system that prevents a fall.

PPE used for safety at height is categorised as type III (protection against mortal danger). As such it must be certified to European Standards by an independent testing house. This gives rise to some limitations as to which equipment is suitable in different circumstances, although users should note that certification does not generally take account of additional rescue loads. Where equipment is intended for rescue purposes its suitability must be further assessed through a risk assessment of its use in relation to rescue situations

1.3.6 The Provision and Use of Work Equipment Regulations 1998 (PUWER)

PUWER 98 applies to the provision and use of all work equipment, including that used for work at height. It places requirements on duty holders to provide suitable work equipment, information, instructions and training. The primary objective is to ensure that work equipment should not result in health and safety risks, regardless of its age, condition or origin.

1.3.7 Lifting Operations and Lifting Equipment Regulations 1998 (LOLER)

All work activities that involve lifting a load come within the scope of LOLER 1998. 'Lifting equipment' is defined as work equipment for lifting or lowering loads and includes its attachments used for anchoring, fixing or supporting the load. A 'lifting operation' is any operation concerned with the lifting or lowering of a load and the term load includes a person.

LOLER requires 'competent persons' to plan lifting activities, as well as conduct inspections and thorough examinations of all equipment used for lifting at work.

The Regulations consider a competent person to be one who has such appropriate practical and theoretical knowledge and practical experience of lifting equipment as will enable them to select, use, care and maintain lifting equipment and accessories. They must receive adequate information, instruction and on the principles of lifting and lifting equipment and be able to account for any limitations on use.

Any person carrying out a thorough examination must have such appropriate practical and theoretical knowledge and experience of the lifting equipment to be thoroughly examined as will enable them to detect defects or weaknesses and to assess their importance in relation to the safety and continued use of the lifting equipment.

1.4 Organisational Roles and Responsibilities

1.4.1 Fire and Rescue Authorities

The Integrated Risk Management Plan (IRMP) will set out the range of risks that individual Fire and Rescue Authorities will consider when developing their plan. Work at Height should be identified as a hazard in the IRMP process and Fire and Rescue Authorities will then allocate suitable and sufficient resources to allow such work to be planned, supervised and carried out safely.

1.4.2 Principal Officers/Brigade Managers

On behalf of Fire and Rescue Authorities, principal officers/brigade managers must consider the outcome of strategic risk assessments to establish the extent to which they will undertake work at height.

The outcomes of systematic risk assessments must then be considered in order to inform decisions on which work activities can be undertaken, outsourced or can't be resourced. This will help define the service's requirement to provide work at height equipment alongside appropriate training and the development of relevant procedures.

In making these decisions it will be necessary to:

- Take account of all relevant statutory provisions.
- Establish policies, set priorities and define safe systems of work.
- Ensure the provision of appropriate equipment, information, training and supervision.
- Review policies and procedures and revise as appropriate.
- Ensure suitable and sufficient resources are available to provide safe systems of work.

1.4.3 Management of Work at Height Activities

All managers with a responsibility for organizing, planning and supervising work at height must be competent. Specific work at height responsibilities should be included in health and safety policies and job descriptions appropriate to the needs of the service.

When a decision is taken to undertake specialist technical rope-working activities, an officer should be nominated to take overall management responsibility for the activity. The duties of the responsible officer will include:

- Formulation, evaluation, review and modification of service procedures.
- Monitoring records of training, equipment use and equipment testing.
- Evaluation of new equipment and procedures and identification of their suitability for use in the brigade.
- Representing the service in rope working matters at local, regional and national level.
- Supervising dealings with rope working equipment and training suppliers.

The officer nominated to take overall management responsibility for rope work activities must receive such training as is necessary to provide the level of knowledge, skills and understanding required by the role.

1.4.3.1 Co-operation with other emergency services/contractors/responsible persons

Fire and rescue authorities must ensure that planning for work at height takes account of circumstances where work may be undertaken in conjunction with other emergency services, agencies or contractors.

Planning and risk assessments should be jointly undertaken and procedures will need to define who has overall responsibility at the work site. The regulations are clear in that employers have responsibility for work at height by their employees and any other person under their control, to the extent of that control. This will apply, for example, to contractors working on fire service premises or representatives from other agencies working within an inner cordon.

1.4.3.2   Duties of employees

Employees must report to their supervisor any activity or defect relating to work at height which is likely to endanger the safety of themselves or any other person. Work equipment or safety devices provided for work at height must be used in accordance with:

- Instructions on use which have been provided.
- Training in the use of the work equipment or safety device.

1.5   Key Hazards and Risks

The hazards and risks associated with working at height arise from the Equipment and its use, the nature of the work undertaken, the work site and prevailing environmental conditions. Each hazard may give rise to one or more risks, with a range of control measures, as listed in the tables below.

Key Hazards and Risks
Table A: Equipment

Hazards	Consequences	Mitigating Control Measures
• Unsuitable equipment. • Incorrect use of equipment. • Damaged equipment. • Incorrect assessment of loading. • Excessive force applied to equipment. • Failure of knot or securing system. • Failure of anchor or belay system. • Entanglement with equipment. • Person being raised or lowered striking or entangling with obstructions . • Uncontrolled descent. • Descent or being lowered off the end of a rope. • Suspension trauma.	Death. Crushing, asphyxiation and impact related injuries. Entrapment of body parts. Falls or impact from falling objects. Cuts, bruises etc. Rope friction burns. Overload of equipment. Failure or malfunction of equipment or work systems. Damage to equipment.	Effective procurement management system. Appropriate labelling. Provision of suitable and sufficient information. Training. Pre-use checks and inspections. Safe system of work. Correct use of appropriate equipment. Secondary safety system. Inspection and thorough examination of equipment. Appropriate cleaning, drying, transport and storing of equipment. Records of use, examinations, maintenance and testing. Planning and effective supervision of lifting and lowering operations. Correct selection and use of anchor points. Provision of energy absorbing equipment. Stopper knot tied in end of rope. Use of deviation. Effective communications.

Key Hazards and Risks
Table B: Nature of the Work

Hazards	Consequences	Mitigating Control Measures
<ul><li>Working at height.</li><li>Access and egress to the work area.</li><li>Duration of the work activity.</li><li>Casualty/victim handling.</li><li>Physiological effects.</li><li>Psychological effects.</li><li>Working with other agencies.</li><li>Members of the public.</li></ul>	Falls or impact from falling objects. Fatigue. Entrapment and crushing. Vertigo, motion sickness. Strains, sprains and other manual handling injuries. Medical contamination by blood or other fluids. Fatigue, cold, hypothermia, heat stress, dehydration. Unpredictable reaction to exposure. Potential for confusion/conflict.	Selection of personnel with physical fitness and mental aptitude for the task. Training. Provision of suitable and sufficient information. Effective supervision. Selection and use of suitable PPE, including clothing. Use of work restraint, fall arrest or work positioning equipment. Secondary safety system. Work area management, including provision of hazard zones. Use of ladders and aerial appliances. Minimum numbers of personnel committed. Appropriate first aid training. Adequate welfare arrangements. Pre-planning and liaison.

Key Hazards and Risks
Table C: Work Site and Prevailing Environmental Conditions

Hazards	Consequences	Mitigating Control Measures
• Sloping, loose or slippery surfaces. • Uneven ground. • Fragile roofs. • Darkness and inadequate lighting. • Presence of corrosive or harmful substances. • Microwave, RF, laser or other electromagnetic transmissions. • Sharp or protruding edges and abrasive surfaces. • Movement or failure of the structure or work area. • Vehicle movements in the work area. • Unstable working platforms. • Lightning. • Rain. • Cold weather conditions. • Hot weather conditions. • Wind.	Falls or impact from falling objects. Slips and trips. Struck by vehicle. Damage of textile based equipment leading to equipment failure. Eye injuries, temporary blinding, burns. Entanglement of clothing or equipment. Obscured surfaces. Impaired/reduced vision. Windblown material. Increased background noise. Exposure to cold, hypothermia, wind chill.	Selection of personnel with physical fitness and mental aptitude for the task. Training. Provision of suitable and sufficient information. Effective supervision. Work area management, including provision of hazard zones. Selection and use of suitable PPE, including clothing. Sufficient, well sited and effective lighting. Use of work restraint equipment or fall arrest equipment. Use of ladders or crawling boards and information relating to fragility. Adequate welfare arrangements. Avoid entering path of laser / microwave transmissions. Maintain safe distance from electromagnetic transmissions. RF monitoring equipment. Use of rope protectors, pads or edge rollers. Cessation of operations.

Key Hazards and Risks
Table D: Equipment Use

Hazards	Consequences	Mitigating Control Measures
<ul><li>Inappropriate use of equipment.</li><li>Overload of equipment or excessive force being applied to the equipment.</li><li>Failure of knot or securing system.</li><li>Failure of anchor or belay system.</li><li>Entanglement with equipment.</li><li>Person being raised or lowered striking or entangling with obstructions.</li><li>Uncontrolled descent through equipment failure or operator error.</li><li>Descent or being lowered off the end of a rope.</li><li>Suspension trauma.</li><li>Inadequate communications.</li></ul>	Fall or being struck by falling object. Damage to equipment. Catastrophic equipment failure. Entanglement/ entrapment with equipment resulting in crush, amputation or other physical injury. Crushing, asphyxiation and impact related injuries, death. Rope friction burns.	Planning and effective supervision of lifting and lowering operations. Correct use of appropriate equipment. Training. Use of back-up safety device kept as high as possible. Use of separate anchor point for each rope. Provision of energy absorbing equipment. Stopper knot tied in end of rope. Use of stretchers. Use of deviation. Effective communications.

1.6   Developing Safe Systems of Work

1.6.1   Clothing

Planning for work at height activities should include consideration of appropriate clothing for all reasonably foreseeable circumstances. In some cases the clothing provided may be classified as PPE whilst on other occasions it may be part of a clothing system to ensure comfort to the individual in a particular working environment.

Although standard fire-fighting PPE is suitable for many activities undertaken whilst working at height, more technical activities involving rope access or rope rescue, may require clothing that is specific to the activity. This may involve different levels of protection from environmental factors or clothing to facilitate comfort and free movement.

When assessing the suitability of clothing and PPE provided for use during work at height, its compatibility with other elements of PPE, particularly harnesses and associated equipment, should be specifically considered.

1.6.2   Before Work at Height

1.6.2.1   Policy and Planning

Injuries can be caused by falls from relatively low heights. Injury statistics show that falls from head height or lower account for two-thirds of major injury accidents caused by falls. It cannot be assumed that little or nothing need be done to prevent falls, therefore risk assessments must be completed before performing work at height. A risk assessment, undertaken by a competent person will identify the health and safety risks and appropriate control measures, for incorporation into standard operating procedures and training.

When identifying capacity and capability appropriate to hazards, each fire and rescue service should undertake a risk assessment to determine the issues relating to work at height relevant to the risk profile of the area in which they may respond. This will allow decisions to be made on the balance between core working at height skills and the need for more specialised systems. In carrying out these assessments, generic and site specific risks must be evaluated.

Generic hazards may include tall buildings, masts, pylons, cranes or scaffolding, tall chimneys, cliffs, steep embankments or dams, deep shafts or wells, agricultural or other silos, chair lifts, gondolas, cable cars, trees, etc.

Specific sites – such as large buildings or industrial complexes, known recreational or climbing venues, theme parks, or potential suicide sites may include the presence of one or more of the above generic hazards.

The factors to be considered in the risk assessment should include:

Safe Place
- Weather and environment – what effects will the weather and environmental conditions have on outdoor work at height?
- Conditions on site – are the ground conditions stable and secure enough to support a ladder or aerial appliance?
- Stability of the working environment – is it a fragile or unstable surface?
- Danger from falling objects – is there a risk of people being hit by falling objects?

Safe Process
- Task to be performed – is it operational, training or routine maintenance?
- Most suitable equipment for the task after a risk assessment – should a ladder, rope rescue equipment, or aerial appliance be used?
- Duration of the task – is it a single task of short duration or protracted working?
- Frequency with which the task needs to be performed – is it a one off, or an everyday occurrence?
- Risks that arise from pre and post use of the equipment – for example is there additional risk in pitching a ladder?
- Rescue procedures if something goes wrong – what contingency arrangements need to be in place?

Safe Person
- Numbers of people required to undertake the task – is it a single person or larger numbers?
- The total exposure of all the workers involved to risk, and the degree of that risk – how many people are exposed to the risk and how severe is it?
- Competence of the crews and the level of supervision required – are they in training, under development or assessed as competent?

A management system should be developed for work at height with supervision that is proportionate to the risk and:

- Takes account of the experience and capability of the people involved in the work. For example trainee firefighters would require a greater degree of supervision than a competent crew.
- Includes a process of briefing personnel to ensure they are aware of hazards and specific circumstances in which they might have to ask for further assistance.
- Puts in place a rescue plan to cater for emergencies which considers additional risks to rescuers and, any need for additional resources.
- Ensures that working practices are modified to provide systems of work that minimise risk to health or safety during the emergency phase of an incident in inclement weather.

1.6.2.2 Liaison with Other Agencies and Voluntary Organisations

When developing work at height procedures, it is essential that the fire and rescue service liaises with other agencies, commercial and voluntary organisations within their area that may already provide a similar service, or with whom the fire and rescue service may be expected to work at incidents. This is particularly important in the case of mountain or cave rescue associations who are likely to have specialist expertise, which may be of benefit to the FRS. Where such organisations exist, a working protocol should be developed with local teams.

In the case of fire and rescue services whose area incorporates coastline or estuaries, close cooperation with the Maritime and Coastguard Agency (MCA) is essential during pre-planning for coastal and littoral incidents. CFOA and the MCA have agreed an outline Memorandum of Understanding for rescue on cliffs or from littoral areas.

1.6.2.3 Industry Liaison

Sector specific guidance for work at height is produced for a number of different industries.

Businesses that undertake work at height have a specific duty to prepare plans to rescue their own workers in the event of an emergency. Where a business wishes to include the fire and rescue service as part of their emergency arrangements they should formally agree this expectation before including it in their emergency procedures. Fire and rescue services may wish to consider whether such arrangements should be classified as chargeable special services.

1.6.2.4 Selection and Training of Personnel

No person shall engage in any work at height activity unless they are competent to do so, or are under supervision during training. This includes planning, organising, supervision, selection and use of equipment as well as carrying out the activity itself. This principle applies to both staff directly engaged in work at height and relevant managers.

There is a general requirement for all employees who may need to work at height to be able to work safely when doing so. More specialist work at height, which involves activities in high and exposed situations, places particular demands on individuals, such that some people are not able to cope with the psychological or physiological stressors involved. Personnel selected as members of specialist teams must have an appropriate attitude and aptitude for such work. Selection and training processes should take account of:

- Medical, physical and psychological fitness to work in high and exposed locations.
- The need for specialist operators to work in difficult environments out of sight of their supervisors.

- The need for trainees to be carefully monitored.
- The need for individuals who experience psychological difficulties to be identified during training and to be given the opportunity to withdraw or be withdrawn from specialist operations.

See Figure 1.1.

Occupational health screening facilities can assist in this area. In view of the above, it is unlikely that fire and rescue services will consider that specialist operations of this nature should be compulsory.

1.6.3 During Work at Height

1.6.3.1 Planning and Command

The nature and urgency of the task to be undertaken must be considered when determining

Figure 1.1 A photograph showing a typical location for rope working, high and exposed.

appropriate control measures. Individual protection may be appropriate for work at height involving rescue or other **urgent** operational activities to protect human life or control a deteriorating situation in the early phase of an incident. Consideration should, however, always be given to collective protection systems particularly when urgent activities have been completed.

All work at height operations must be adequately supervised as appropriate to the nature and complexity of the situation. When implementing a safe system of work, ongoing dynamic risk assessments should be proportionate to the level of risk involved and consider:

- Alternative ways of working.
- Time imperatives for action and duration of activities.
- Competence of personnel relative to the complexity of the intended activities.
- Availability of suitable resources.
- Environmental conditions.
- Access and egress.
- Organisation of the work area.
- Supervision.
- Communication requirements.
- Safety management systems.
- Emergency Procedures.
- Control measures appropriate to the number of people exposed to the risk.

Issues identified in the dynamic risk assessment should be clearly communicated to all personnel involved through a safety briefing before operations commence.

When rope work systems are operated by specialist technical rope work teams, the incident command structure should include supervision by competent specialist personnel. Depending on the complexity and duration of the incident, a suitable management structure may include a:

- Rope sector commander.
- Work at height supervisor.
- Rope safety officer.

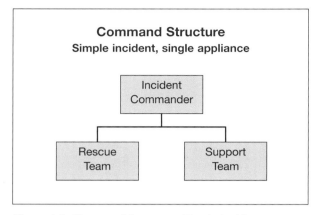

Figure 1.2 Command Structure: Simple incident, single appliance.

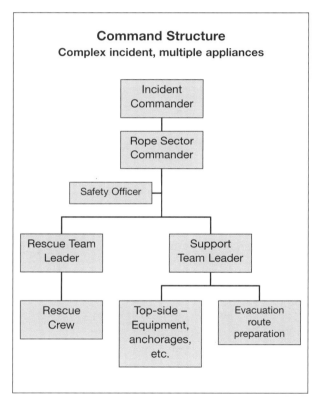

Figure 1.3 Command Structure: Complex incident, multiple appliances.

1.6.3.2 Hazard Zones

To minimise the risk of injury to personnel and members of the public, hazard zones must be established, cordoned off and operated in line with inner cordon principles. This must include the working location and areas of risk above and below when:

● Individuals are working at height and there is a risk of a fall likely to cause injury.
● Individuals are at risk of being struck by falling objects.
● Rope is being used to haul, lift or lower loads, or for working at height.

Hazard zones should be established in accordance with the following principles:

● The hazard zone must be large enough to enable the risk to be controlled. The size may be influenced by available space, nature of risk, high winds or other adverse conditions. On stable ground and in good weather conditions, a minimum distance of three metres from an unprotected edge may be considered appropriate.
● The boundary of the zone must be effectively indicated, providing a physical barrier and illuminated during hours of darkness. Consideration should be given to the need for the boundary of the zone to be staffed or identified by hazard warning signs.
● The number of personnel within the hazard zone should be kept to the minimum.
● All individuals who enter a hazard zone must be fully briefed and correctly protected with appropriate PPE.
● Rope anchor and belay points should, where possible, be placed outside the hazard zone.
● Casualty holding areas and equipment dumps should be placed outside the hazard zone.

See Figure 1.4.

1.6.3.3 Inter-Service Liaison and Control of Operations

The FRS will always maintain a high level of operational responsibility and control at any incident where there is a requirement to save

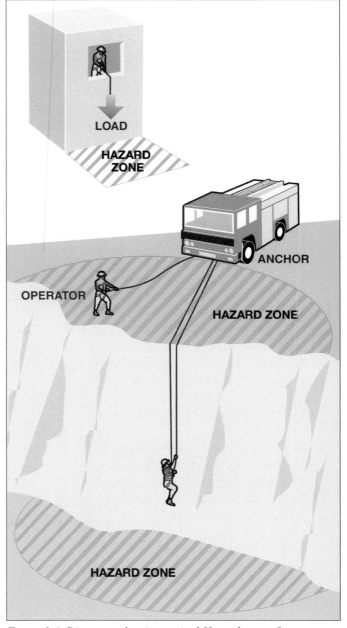

Figure 1.4 Diagrams showing typical Hazard zones for:
  Hauling or lowering equipment.
  Cliff or crag rescue.

endangered life. This is particularly so when activities involve work at height, as the fire and rescue service generally provides the primary resources to implement safe systems of work. It also frequently assists other agencies that may need to work at height and in such circumstances manages overall scene safety. Control reverts solely to the police when an incident involves suspected terrorist activities. In either circumstance it is imperative that clear communications exist between agencies to establish clarity of what needs to be done, how it needs to be done and all associated risks.

The location and potential exposure of places of work at height means evidence may be lost through environmental influences. Consideration should be given to taking active measures that protect a scene of investigation, although such measures must be proportionate to the risk encountered and remain within the boundaries of safe working practices.

1.6.4 Post Work at Height

1.6.4.1 Debriefing

All work at height activities should be followed by an appropriate level of debriefing, with other agencies involved as appropriate. Any significant outcomes should be documented and then used to review systems and equipment, making changes as necessary.

1.6.4.2 Monitoring and Reviewing

Work at height systems should be regularly monitored and reviewed to ensure they continue to reflect good practice, service standards and local requirements. Both active and reactive review systems should be used.

1.6.4.3 Auditing

Audit processes should enable fire and rescue services to reinforce, maintain and improve their ability to reduce risks associated with work at height. The audit process should seek to ensure that:

- Appropriate training, equipment, procedures and supervision are in place.
- Staff demonstrate competence for work at height.
- Staff understand their legal responsibilities for work at height.
- Adequate risk controls exist and they reflect the nature and complexity of work at height activities.
- Fire and rescue services improve performance and respond to change.
- Systems include operational audit of work at height activities.

Safe Work at Height

Chapter 2 – Operational Practices

2.1   General Techniques

Work should not be carried out at height if there is a reasonably practicable means to carry out the work safely, otherwise than at height. Where work is carried out at height, measures should be taken to prevent a fall. Where it is not practicable to prevent the risk of a fall, the distance and consequence of a fall must be minimised. Work at height involves a series of specific considerations, overlapping techniques and procedures including:

- Collective safeguards comprising:
  - Nets.
  - Air bags.
  - Bean bags.
  - Mats and other soft landing systems.
- Individual protection by:
  - Work restraint.
  - Fall arrest.
  - Work positioning.
- Access techniques with:
  - MEWPs.
  - Working platforms.
  - Ladders.
  - Ropes, harnesses and associated equipment.
- Systems of work to control:
  - Falling objects and Hazard zones.
  - Anchors and anchor systems.
  - Securing equipment and other items.
  - Lifting, lowering and hauling.
  - Securing casualties and performing rescues from height.

2.1.1   Collective Safeguards for Arresting Falls

Collective safeguards comprise nets, air bags, beans bags, mats and other soft landing systems. These systems are not generally appropriate for fire and rescue service operations, although their use may be appropriate in training or routine work environments. They are increasingly being adopted as a safety measure by industry, so it is likely that fire and rescue service personnel may find such measures already in place when attending an incident. Normal service safety provision by the use of PPE can be considered the most appropriate way to manage risk, although in certain limited circumstances pre-installed collective safeguards for arresting falls my be considered for inclusion in the safety measures taken. Fire and rescue service personnel are unlikely to possess the competences required to assess the suitability and effectiveness of these systems, so specialist on-site advice must be taken before relying on them at an incident. **Collective safeguards that have already been subjected to an impact should not be considered to provide suitable protection for fire and rescue service personnel. In such circumstances personal protection systems should be provided for rescuers.**

Collective safeguards for fall arrest may be considered when it is not appropriate to prevent a fall occurring by either collective or personal protection systems. They must be strong enough to safely arrest a fall, be securely attached to suitable anchors, remain stable during any subsequent rescue and must not, in themselves, cause injury.

Safety netting is generally the preferred collective safeguard for fall arrest used in industry as it does not rely on individual user discipline to guarantee acceptable safety standards. See Figure 2.1.

The following points are considered industry good practice when using safety nets:

- Nets should be installed by a competent rigger and be as close as possible beneath the work area to minimise the distance of any fall and withstand a person falling onto them (2 metres is considered the maximum safe fall). There must be at least 3 metres clearance below the net and proper installation should be confirmed by the issue of a handover certificate.

- For a net to be considered safe to use, it must be attached to a structure with appropriate capacity, have no gaps and any joins between nets must have an overlap of at least 2 metres.
- A visual inspection should be undertaken before safety nets are used.
- The following activities are considered unsafe:
  - Walking in, or jumping into the net.
  - Storing equipment or materials in the net.
  - Tampering with or adjusting the net an attachment.
- Ensure a rescue plan including any rescue equipment is in place before commencing work.
- The area underneath safety netting should be included in the hazard zone.

Air bags, bean bags and mats provide suitable collective safeguards for arresting falls when they can be placed close to the working level in order to minimise the consequences of a fall from height. They should be appropriately anchored, stable and if they distort on impact should afford sufficient clearance to prevent injury. A risk assessment should consider the suitability of this equipment if the fall to the air bags, bean bag or mat is greater than 2 metres. See Figure 2.2.

Figure 2.1 Safety nets on construction site.
(Photo: Health and Safety Executive)

Figure 2.2 Air bags on construction site.
(Photo: Health and Safety Executive)

2.1.2 Individual Protection

Individual protection can be achieved in one of three ways:

- Work restraint.
- Fall arrest.
- Work positioning.

The most appropriate method of individual protection must be determined through a risk assessment of each work environment and the circumstances of the activity to be undertaken.

This list indicates the hierarchy normally used during operational activities, but in other circumstances work positioning may generally be considered before fall arrest.

When making decisions about the use of individual protection systems and the need for and levels of PPE, it is relevant to note that accidents involving falls occur more frequently during the latter stages of incidents than during the initial period of emergency activity. This is considered to be because individuals have an increased awareness of danger during the early and urgent stages of activity, but that such awareness reduces as the incident progresses.

2.1.2.1 Work Restraint

The objective of work restraint (or travel restriction) is to restrict an individual's movement so that access to any location where there is a risk of a fall from a height is not possible. Work restraint equipment is not designed to sustain high

Work Restraint – Example 1

A pump operator working adjacent to a dockside could be secured to a suitable point at the rear of the appliance preventing them from reaching the dock edge.

Figure 2.3 A pump operator at dockside in work restraint.

Work Restraint – Example 2

A fire fighter working in any location with unguarded edges from which there is a risk of a fall that could cause injury can be easily protected by the provision of a waist belt or harness, attached to a suitable anchor point by a rope that is shorter than the distance between the anchor and the edge.

Figure 2.4 Firefighter working near the edge of a flat roof.

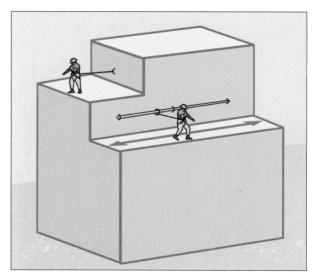

Figure 2.5 *Work Restraint – Technique using PPE to prevent personnel moving into an area of fall potential.*

Figure 2.6 *Photo of a fall arrest system providing safety when accessing a shaft via a fixed vertical ladder.*

Figure 2.7 *Fall Arrest - Technique using PPE to safely arrest a fall.*

shock loads and is unsuitable for work positioning or fall arrest situations.

Equipment Selection for work restraint

The minimum system required to achieve the necessary restriction on travel will be:

- A suitable waist belt or harness.
- A rope or lanyard.
- A reliable anchor point.

The rope or lanyard should be adjusted for length, so that once connected it is impossible for the individual to reach the edge, thus removing the risk of a fall. Adjustment may be managed either by the individual being protected or by a second person operating a rope control device attached to the anchor.

2.1.2.2 Fall Arrest

Fall arrest systems are designed for use in situations where the risk of a fall likely to cause injury exists.

If circumstances demand that individuals operate in a position where a fall resulting in injury could occur, then suitable fall arrest equipment must be used. Although the primary hazard is that of falling a distance likely to cause an injury, the potential and likely consequences of a falling person striking adjacent objects or surfaces should also be assessed

before commencing work. The relevant standard for a complete fall arrest system is EN 363 and it should be assembled from component parts that comply with their own individual standards (e.g. a energy absorbing element to BS EN 355).

Fall Factors

When choosing equipment for fall arrest it is important to understand the effect of fall factors. Work systems should be developed to minimise the fall factor and systems that give a fall factor which exceeds one should not be used unless unavoidable. High fall factors, with potential high impact forces can be associated with an increased risk of injury and damage to equipment. The examples given below illustrate the principle of fall factors in the working environment.

Fall Factors – Example 1

An individual working on a vertical ladder wearing a full body harness is attached to the ladder by a one-metre lanyard. If the individual falls from a position where the attachment point of the lanyard to the ladder is 1 metre below the attachment point to the harness, the total resulting fall will be 2 metres. The fall factor is calculated by comparing the length of the fall with the amount of rope.

$$\text{Fall Factor} = \frac{\text{Height of Fall}}{\text{Length of Rope in the System}}$$

In this situation the fall factor is calculated as 2 metres (fall) divided by 1 metre (rope or lanyard), giving a fall factor of 2.

Figure 2.8 (near right) Diagram of start position showing distances.

Figure 2.9 (far right) Diagram of finish position showing distances.

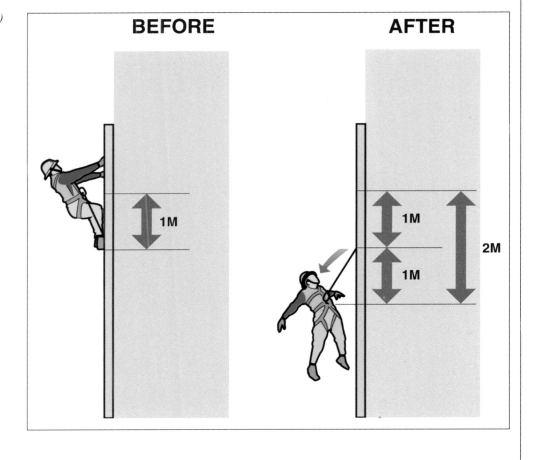

Fall Factors – Example 2

If the same individual falls from a position where the attachment point of the lanyard to the ladder is at the same height as the attachment point of the lanyard to the harness, the resulting fall will be 1 metre. The fall factor is again calculated by comparing the length of the fall with the amount of rope in the system.

In this situation, therefore, the fall factor is calculated as 1 metre (fall) divided by 1 metre (rope or lanyard), giving a fall factor of 1.

Figure 2.10 (near right) Diagram of start position showing distances.

Figure 2.11 (far right) Diagram of finish position showing distances.

BEFORE AFTER

1M OF ROPE

1M

Fall Factors – Example 3

An individual being belayed from above whilst ascending a vertical ladder. The individual is 9 metres below the belay point but the belay rope is slack and there are 10 metres of rope between the belay point and the individual. If the individual falls from this position the resulting fall will be 1 metre. The fall factor is again calculated by comparing the length of the fall with the amount of rope in the system.

In this situation the fall factor is calculated as 1 metre (fall) divided by 10 metres (rope), giving a fall factor of one tenth.

Figure 2.12 (near right) Diagram of start position with individual on ladder showing distances and slack rope.

Figure 2.13 (far right) Diagram of finish position with individual suspended showing distances and tight rope.

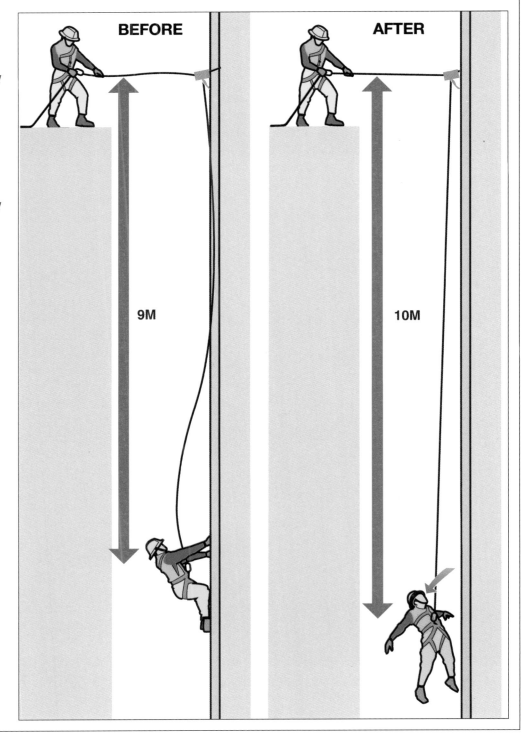

A lower fall factor results in a lower force with a lower shock loading transferred to both the anchor and the individual at the point of fall arrest. In any fall arrest situation dynamic ropes or energy absorbing systems should be used to reduce the effect of high fall factors by stretching as weight is applied during a fall, thereby reducing the transferred forces. When working with dynamic rope or energy absorbing lanyards, it is essential to ensure that an adequate clearance height is available below the scene of operations due to the extension of the system as the fall is arrested.

Equipment Selection for fall arrest
Equipment used for fall arrest is designed to halt a fall and reduce the impact forces generated in doing so. In order to reduce the energy of a fall, excess energy must be absorbed and dissipated within the fall arrest system, therefore a suitable fall arrest system will include:

- A fall arrest harness complying with BS EN361.
- A energy absorbing element.
- A connecting rope or lanyard.
- An effective anchor.

Figure 2.14 Photo of a fire fighter being belayed down a slope where a system is required to prevent them from falling but is not required to support their weight.

A fall arrest system may also be used to provide protection where an individual needs to work on a sloping surface. Such a system might incorporate a single top belayed rope and harness system such as that shown below. This system only provides fall protection for an individual moving into position to carry out a given task; it does not provide a means to support the individual's weight. See Figure 2.14.

2.1.2.3 Work Positioning

When attending any incident where individuals must be supported in tension or suspension to carry out work or affect a rescue, suitable work positioning equipment must be provided. Unlike work restraint or fall arrest, people operating in these situations are totally dependent on the rope system to support their weight and to prevent them falling.

When considering the need to provide work positioning systems, the following principles must be applied:

- Work positioning systems should always include a primary system, from which the individual is suspended and a separate safety or backup system that will come into operation automatically should the primary fail for any reason.
- A safe system of work will be one where the failure of a single component or a single error on the part of the operator will not result in an uncontrolled fall. The term 100% redundancy is sometimes used to illustrate this concept. In order to provide 100% redundancy, no single item of equipment (other than an approved harness) should be relied on anywhere within the system.
- Separate anchor points should be used, unless only one anchor is available, AND it is unquestionably reliable. Separate attachments to that single anchor should still be used for the primary and back-up systems.
- Work positioning harnesses complying with BS EN358 must not be used for fall arrest situations unless they also comply with BS EN361 and suitable energy absorbing elements are included in the work system.

Selection of equipment for work positioning
A work positioning system must include:

- A sit harness or full body harness complying with BS EN358.
- An effective anchor.
- A connecting rope and rope control device. or
- A suitable lanyard system.

When work positioning systems are used in conjunction with breathing apparatus, a full body harness with a high attachment point must be provided to maintain the operator in an upright position.

In situations where it is envisaged that a harness may be worn for extended periods, it should incorporate design and construction features that will ensure the comfort of the wearer in suspension. This may include the provision of a work seat.

Figure 2.15 Example of a work positioning system in use above a silo.

2.2 Access techniques

2.2.1 Working Platforms (General)

Key considerations relating to the use of working platforms include:

AVOID
- Overloading.
- Use in adverse/windy conditions other than for immediate operational need.

PREVENT
- Movement with persons or materials on the platform.
- Climbing up the outside.
- Use of ladders, step ladders, boxes, etc. on top to extend the height.
- Use if any components are damaged.
- Use on soft ground.

MITIGATE
- Always carry out a pre-use check.
- Only use towers that have been properly erected by a competent person (level, vertical, all components present and tied if necessary).
- Only move or use towers if you have received the relevant training or are being supervised by a competent person.
- Follow the manufacturer's instructions for use.
- Always check that all wheels are locked and the tower is the correct height to allow access to the work.
- Check and ensure outriggers/stabilisers or ties are in place as per the manufacturer's instruction.
- Only move by applying effort as near the base as possible.

2.2.2 Scaffolding and Access Towers

Scaffolding and access towers may provide the supporting structure for a work platform which is more stable and provides a safer work environment than can be achieved by working from a ladder or a harness in suspension. The boundary between scaffolding and access towers is not clearly defined and some systems that may appear to be scaffolding are technically considered to be access towers. Some general guidance is, however, provided for fire and rescue services that wish to provide systems for their own use.

Figure 2.16 Example of a working platform.

Scaffolding or access tower erection requires specific training to:

- Ensure competence.
- Allow recognition of when and where scaffolding can be erected.
- Ensure erection, use, maintenance, and dismantling is carried out safely.

Access towers must be secure, with stabilisers in place and any wheels locked, before use. Any plans to use jets from a working platform erected on scaffolding or an access tower must take account of the destabilising effect created by jet reaction. Aerial appliances, which are specifically designed for this activity, may provide a more appropriate solution.

If there is a requirement to move an access tower, care should be taken to ensure:

- No person or items are on the platform.
- Any overhead obstructions or power lines are avoided.
- There are no dips or holes in the floor surface.

In circumstances where scaffolding or access towers are already erected at an incident location, guidance should be sought from the competent person on site and a risk assessment must be undertaken as to its suitability for any planned use by fire and rescue service personnel.

FRS policies relating to contractors working on their premises should specify safe working requirements for scaffolding and access towers.

2.2.3 Mobile Elevated Work Platforms (MEWPs)

Aerial appliances used in a wide range of industries are collectively known as MEWPS and can be effectively used to provide a safe means of working at height. FRS aerial appliances fall into this category of equipment and when operated by competent persons provide a safe work environment. The precautions for safe work from an aerial appliance include:

- Guard rails round the edge of the cage to stop the user falling.
- Toe-boards round the edge of the platform.
- Use of stability devices, e.g. jacks.
- Use of work restraint, work positioning or fall arrest systems with approved anchor points.

A safe system of work should be in place that includes:

- Planning the job to be aware of all hazards, including those from overhead obstructions and passing traffic.
- Use of competent operator(s).
- Use of appropriate harnesses and associated systems.
- Instruction to the crews about safety issues.
- Instructions in emergency procedures, such as evacuation in the event of power failure.

Aerial appliances are also lifting equipment for lifting people as defined by LOLER. Fire and rescue services should therefore ensure that an aerial appliance has a thorough examination by a competent person once every 6 months or in accordance with an examination scheme drawn up by a competent person. Routine maintenance should be performed in accordance with the manufacturer's instructions and advice from a competent person.

2.2.4 Continuity of Means of Protection

It may be necessary in certain circumstances to remove guardrails, fencing and other means of protection for short periods. The regulations make it clear that this is permissible under the following conditions:

- Removal is only for the time and extent necessary for the job, then the barrier is replaced. and
- The work is not done unless there is some other safeguard, e.g. a safety net or work restraint system.

Measures to protect workers while the task is carried out could include safe systems of work (or permit to work systems where appropriate) including the provision of a fall arrest system, limiting access to specified people and ensuring those performing the task are provided with adequate information, training and supervision.

If regular access or egress is required, such as with aerial appliance cages it may be more appropriate to provide gates or bars. In all cases the gap in the protection should be minimised and replaced immediately the operation has finished.

2.2.5 Portable Ladders

Portable ladders, including extension, step and roof ladders, are frequently required for fire and rescue service operational activities. Specific guidance on practical techniques for their use is included in The Fire and Rescue Service Manual, Volume 4 Fire Service Training, Foundation Training and Development. When determining the suitability of ladders for any task, the considerations listed in Regulation 7 must be taken into account and the following aspects specifically considered:

- Is the activity urgent? Is there an imperative to save human life or control a deteriorating situation? Would waiting for an alternative means of access compromise the outcome?

- Are there alternative means of access and egress that avoid the need to use ladders?
- Do the working and environmental conditions increase the risk of using a ladder?
- Do the weather conditions increase the risk of using a ladder?
- What is the expected duration of use? Is the ladder going to be used as a work platform or solely as a means of access and egress?
- Does the nature and duration of work mean that staff will need relieving?
- Is the ladder selected appropriate for the task?
- Can equipment needed at height be safely carried leaving both hands free for climbing the ladder or does it need to be hauled aloft?
- Is the construction of a sloping roof on which a roof ladder is placed or the construction against which the head of an extension ladder rests strong enough to support the intended load?

2.2.5.1 General Safety During Use

When a decision is made that ladders are appropriate for access or to undertake activities at height, working practices should ensure:

- Non-service portable ladders are not used, as it will be difficult to confirm they are fit for purpose.
- That the surface which a ladder stands on is stable, firm, of sufficient strength and of suitable composition to support the ladder safely.
- The ladder is positioned so that its rounds remain horizontal and it will support the intended load.
- The heel of the ladder is secured to prevent it moving in any direction, by footing the ladder or tying it in place.
- Where appropriate the head of the ladder is secured, e.g. tying the head in to the building.
- Portable ladders are correctly footed by two people to ensure stability when used for rescue or any activity that may exert a directional force (E.G. operating a branch from the head of the ladder).
- Roof and extension ladders can be secured together to prevent movement between them when transferring from one to the other.

- Where possible the ladder should generally be extended sufficiently above the point of landing to provide a handhold when mounting and dismounting. Three clear rounds will generally be sufficient.
- The improvised use of ladders as stepladders, for bridging, as an anchor system for lifting or lowering, or for other similar activities must only be undertaken in accordance with the manufacturer's instructions.

2.2.6 Fixed Ladders

Fixed ladders are frequently found in environments where it is not practical to use fire and rescue service ladders for access. Examples may include ladders found in ships holds, communication masts, sewers, wind generators or fire service training towers.

Fixed ladders with short vertical runs or hooped construction may be used by suitably trained personnel without additional fall prevention precautions being taken, provided only one person is on the ladder at a time. In all other circumstances suitable precautions must be taken to prevent or arrest a fall from the ladder. Specific points to consider include:

- Is the ladder in a location where it is regularly used and inspected?
- If the ladder is not regularly used and inspected does it have obvious signs of corrosion or instability?
- Does the ladder lead into a confined space?
- Are safe landing areas or rest platforms provided at regular intervals?
- Is there sufficient space at the bottom of the ladder for personnel to stand clear?
- On longer runs of vertical ladders, can personnel maintain a sufficient gap to accommodate any fall arrest device employed?

2.2.6.1 Suspended ladders

Suspended ladders, generally of a flexible construction, are manufactured of varying materials including wire, carbon fibre and/or nylon fabric. They are generally used as a temporary means of access and egress being positioned only when in use and where rigid ladders can not be practicably positioned or are not suitable.

When using these ladders the following points should be considered:

- A suitable anchorage is required for the ladder.
- An additional fall arrest system is usually required to protect an individual from the effects of a fall from the ladder.
- Very few types of flexible ladder are able to withstand a shock loading – as such a separate anchor is required for any fall arrest system.
- Where possible, controlling movement of the bottom of the ladder will ensure climbing the ladder is made easier.
- These ladders may be difficult to climb when laid against a surface, unless fitted with spacers to hold them off the surface so that hands and feet can be easily placed on the rounds.
- Care should be taken during positioning to ensure the ladder does not become snagged or twisted.

Within the FRS, use of this type of equipment is generally restricted to specialist teams who have received the appropriate training.

2.2.6.2 Ladders as work platforms

When work is undertaken from a ladder, rather than using it solely as a means of access or egress, it is categorised as a work platform. Ladders should only be used as work platforms where a risk assessment shows that the use of other work equipment is not justified because of either:

- The risk assessment establishes the activity is low risk and the task is of a short duration. or
- There are unalterable features of the work site that preclude the use of more appropriate equipment.

When a ladder is used as a work platform, appropriate measures should be in place to prevent or mitigate the effects of a fall. A leg lock should only be considered appropriate for short duration tasks within easy reach of the ladder, otherwise fall arrest equipment must be used.

Specific points to consider when assessing whether it is appropriate to use a ladder as a work platform include:

- Are alternative safe systems of work available, or should they be introduced following initial actions?
- Can the area be controlled with a hazard zone below the work platform?
- Does the ladder need to be secured to the structure or can stability be maintained by footing?
- Is maintaining a leg-lock suitable for the work to be undertaken or does other provision need to be made to prevent a fall?
- Is the ladder approved for use as a fall arrest anchor and its lateral stability ensured in case of a fall to the side?
- Can an independent anchor be provided for the fall arrest system?
- Can the work be carried out without stretching to a position that could make the ladder or person on it unstable?
- Does the ladder need repositioning to ensure stability during the task?
- What are the manual handling considerations?

2.2.7 Ropes, Harnesses and Associated Equipment

These systems provide effective safe systems of work, but should only be selected when the risk assessment of a work activity identifies that collective methods of protection are unsuitable due to:

- The urgency of need for access to a location at height.
- A limited number of people being exposed to risk.
- The short duration of a work activity.

In circumstances where access is available to an area above the scene of operations and a suitable anchor site can be established, normal work restraint, work positioning or fall arrest techniques should be used. The systems of work generally used when work positioning is selected include those shown in the examples below (see Figures 2.17, 2.18 and 2.19).

Work Positioning Systems – Example 1

Top controlled lower on two ropes, one being the working rope and one the safety rope.

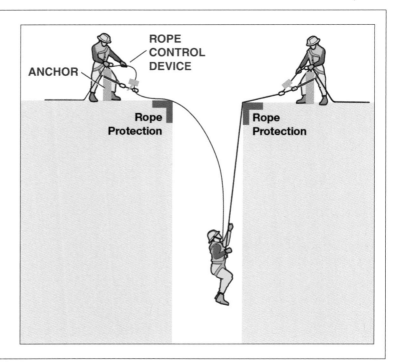

Figure 2.17 Operator being lowered on a working rope with backup provided by a second rope belayed from the top.

Work Positioning Systems – Example 2

Operator-controlled descent on a working rope with a top-belayed safety rope.

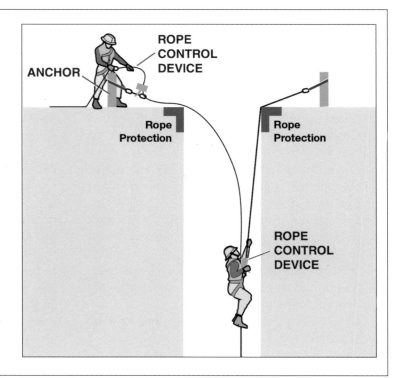

Figure 2.18 Operator descending on a fixed top rope with backup provided by a second rope belayed from the top.

Work Positioning Systems – Example 3

Operator-controlled descent on a working rope with operator-controlled safety device on a separate safety rope.

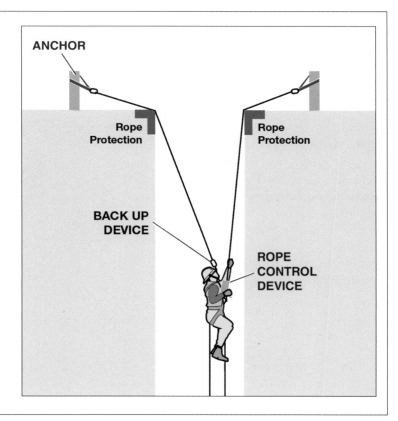

Figure 2.19 Operator descending on a fixed top rope with backup safety device attached to a second fixed rope.

These systems all describe techniques that allow an individual to work using two ropes. In **very exceptional circumstances** where delay could threaten human life or allow a situation to deteriorate quickly there may be a need for an individual to operate with one rope. This may be achieved by either a top controlled lower or operator controlled descent on one working rope.

Using a single rope system should only be considered in extreme situations where inaction would result in serious injury or death to the rescuer or casualty. A suitable and sufficient risk assessment should take place prior to and during all single rope work. Special attention should be given to the suitability of anchors, with all anchors used during single rope work being unquestionably reliable.

Once casualty access and safety has been achieved, unless urgent casualty evacuation is required due to medical reasons, consideration should be given to waiting for the arrival of further equipment and/or personnel to allow the addition of a second system.

The system deemed most suitable will depend on the situation involved, the experience of the individuals involved and the availability of suitably experienced support personnel.

In circumstances where no access is available to a safe location above the work site it will be necessary to employ a 'bottom up' approach. This will generally involve the first operator having to ascend to a point above the scene of operations where suitable anchors may be established.

In order to carry out this process safely, there are two recognised safe climbing methods, using:

● Lanyards or 'cow's tails'.

● Lead climbing techniques.

In either case the individual should trail a second rope, which can be anchored above the work location and provide a more secure system of ascent for subsequent operators.

2.2.7.1　Use of Lanyards

This is a relatively simple system, which involves the use of two lanyards attached to the operator's harness via a suitable energy absorbing device(s) to arrest a fall. It is often used when ascending vertical ladders or climbing open steelwork. The operator attaches the first lanyard as high as possible and then starts to ascend, repositioning each lanyard to a new anchor point as the ascent is made. The operator must ensure that at every point during the climb, at least one of the lanyards is secured to an anchor that will provide protection should a fall occur. (See Figure 2.20.)

Figure 2.20 Diagram showing the use of lanyards.

2.2.7.2 Use of Lead Climbing Techniques

Lead climbing is a technique in which the operator is protected by a rope or ropes, running through intermediate 'running belays' and controlled by a person operating a rope control device at the base of the climb. It is a specialist technique, normally only appropriate for specifically trained and competent rope work technicians.

As the operator ascends, the climbing rope will be attached to a series of intermediate belay points attached to the structure. These 'running belays' may take the form of previously attached anchor points or may be added by the operator as the first ascent takes place (e.g. by placing slings and karabiners around suitable parts of the structure). Each running belay should be able to support the weight of the operator in the event of a fall.

Should a fall occur, movement of the rope would be limited by the rope control device at the base of the climb, thus arresting the operator's fall. (See Figure 2.21.)

When using lead climbing techniques:

●   Dynamic rope or a suitable energy absorbing system must be used to reduce the shock loads that may be generated in the event of a fall. and

●   The degree of extension that will occur during fall arrest must be considered.

2.2.7.3 Recovery or Self -Rescue

Wherever possible the operator should descend to the bottom of the risk area, disconnect from the system and walk to a place of safety. If this is not possible a suitable recovery system must be available. This may include a winching system or some other means by which the operator can ascend the ropes on which they were lowered.

To be completely independent, the operator would need to be additionally equipped with suitable rope control devices to ascend the ropes, thereby having independent control of ascent and descent.

Situations in which this technique is of use would include exiting from a confined space such as a

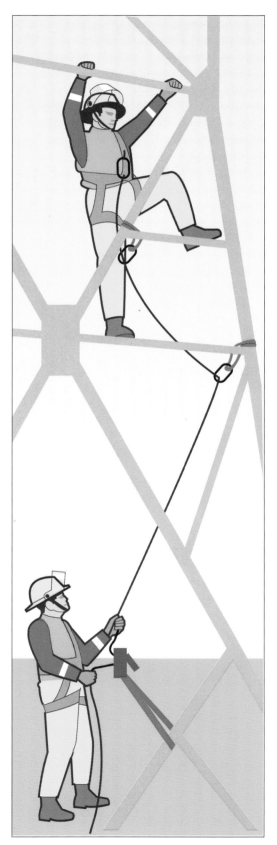

Figure 2.21 Diagram showing the use of lead climbing techniques.

silo or when accompanying a casualty being raised on a separate system.

The use of this technique requires that the operator is competent in changing from a descent mode to an ascent mode and vice versa.

These techniques are considered advanced rope working skills and as such would only be undertaken by competent rope work technicians. (See Figure 2.22.)

2.2.7.4   Highlines and Cableways

Situations occur where obstacles and projections prevent a direct vertical rescue and operators will need to change the angle of descent to prevent operators or casualties from striking these obstructions. Techniques to achieve this include the use of highlines and cableways.

Figure 2.22 A simple 3:1 recovery system in operation.

Highlines

The simplest example of a highline system is the use of a tensioned tag or guy line that allows the descending casualty and/or operator to be lowered at an angle away from a building. In this system, the working rope takes the load and the tag or guy line is used to deviate the angle of descent. This is termed a 'tensioned deviation' system. (See Figure 2.23).

Cableways

In more complex systems, ropes support the rescuer and/or casualty whilst control ropes are used to move them along a planned route. The supporting ropes will be secured at each end and tensioned to provide the required angle of travel. The movement of the rescuer and/or casualty along the supporting ropes is controlled by the use of rope control devices at both ends of the control ropes.

The use of these systems can create extreme loads at the anchor points requiring the use of multiple anchors and/or back up systems. (See Figure 2.24.)

Due to the increased complexity of these systems, many fire and rescue services will see the operation of cableways being restricted to competent rope work technicians.

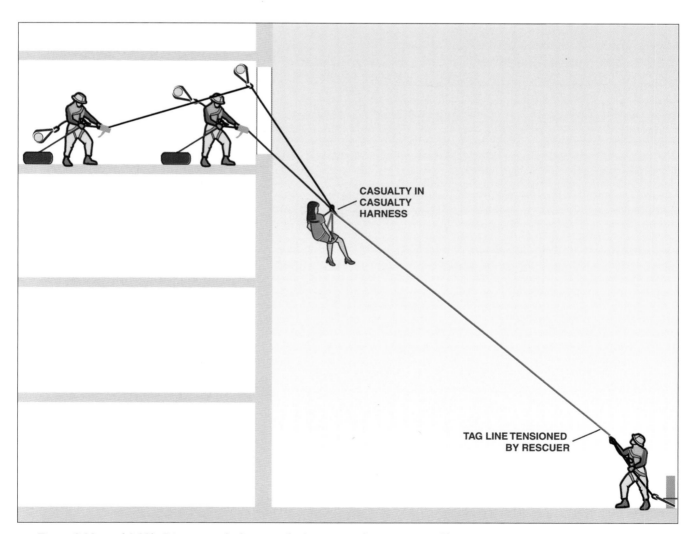

Figure 2.23a and 2.23b Diagrams of a lowering by line system being tensioned by an operator.

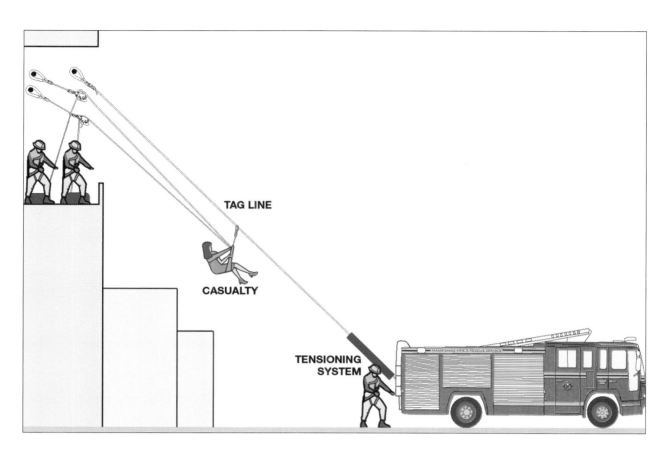

Figure 2.23b
(above)

Figure 2.24 (right)
Aerial cableway
(and detail).

2.3 Systems of Work

2.3.1 Anchors and Anchor Systems

2.3.1.1 General

An anchor can be defined as a safe point or object to which a load may be securely attached. An anchor system includes the anchor **and** the equipment used to connect it to the load or the rope supporting the load.

In all cases the anchor system provides the foundation for rope work operations and is a critical part of any rope system. The anchor system must be **unquestionably reliable**.

2.3.1.2 Anchors

Individual anchors can be divided into two broad categories:

- Natural anchors.

- Artificial anchors.

(a) Natural Anchors
Natural anchors can be described as those furnished by the terrain such as trees and rocks. Care must be taken when selecting natural anchors to ensure that they are substantial and that they are capable of supporting the intended load. In particular, the following points should be considered:

- Rocks and boulders should be assessed prior to being placed under load.
- Trees must be examined carefully to ensure that they are alive, in a sound and healthy condition and deep rooted. Special care should be taken with trees that are growing in shallow soil, such as is found near the edges of cliffs and quarries as they may have inferior root systems.
- To be considered as a reliable anchor, a tree should have a minimum trunk diameter of 15cm and anchors should be secured around the base to reduce leverage.

(b) Artificial Anchors
Artificial anchors are those specifically positioned by the fire service or others to provide an attachment to which ropes may be secured. Artificial anchors can be further divided into:

- Permanent artificial anchors.

- Temporary artificial anchors.

Permanent artificial anchors such as eyebolts are those that are left in place when not in use. These anchors are generally considered reliable, as they have been specifically positioned and constructed for anchorage purposes. They must be proof tested

*Figure 2.25
Photograph of rock being used as an anchor.*

Figure 2.26 *Photo of permanent artificial anchor.*

before first use and re-tested in accordance with the manufacturer's instructions or written scheme of work. They must also be checked on a regular basis both prior to and during use to ensure continued safety. (See Figure 2.26.)

Temporary artificial anchors such as vehicles, ground stakes, steelwork or climbing aids, are objects utilised for anchorage only for the period of use. In many cases they will have other primary functions but their size, weight or location allows them to be used as anchors. These provide by far the majority of anchors for operational fire service use. (See Figure 2.27.)

2.3.1.3 Anchor Systems

Anchor systems may comprise a single anchor, commonly known as a 'single point anchor system' or may incorporate a number of linked anchors, a 'multi-point anchor system'.

In establishing a safe anchor system, consideration should be given to:

● Attachment to anchors.
● Backing up anchors.
● Anchor redundancy.
● Equalisation of anchors.
● Equalising knots and slings.

Figure 2.27 *Photograph of temporary artificial anchors.*

- Extension of a system following failure.
- Divergence of angles in multiple anchor systems.

(a) Attachment to anchors

Consideration can be given to attaching rope directly to certain types of anchors, for example, around the trunks of trees, but this may have a detrimental effect on the long-term durability of the rope. In general, where a connector such as a karabiner or screw link cannot be attached directly to the anchor, a sling or strop should be applied around the anchor. The rope system may then be connected to the sling or strop by suitable connectors, taking care to minimise any side loading or leverage on the anchor.

Looping the sling through itself should be avoided, as this will severely reduce the strength of the sling. Where a single sling is not long enough to go around the anchor it may be extended by another sling or replaced by a rope loop. Slings must be joined using a suitable connector and not connected directly together as this may weaken them due to friction between the slings.

When setting up a 'multi-point' anchor system, the use of a rigging plate should be considered as this provides a well laid out and easily checked system. (See Figure 2.28.)

(b) Backing up anchors

Where the anchor selected is a smooth boulder or tapered metal structure, the direction of pull may cause the sling(s) to slip off the anchor. In this case an additional sling, termed a backup sling, must be provided.

Where an individual single point anchor is of substantial construction and assessed as being unquestionably reliable, it may be used on its own to support a load, that may be attached to the anchor by means of a single sling and connector. Although the anchor is unquestionably reliable, the sling is not and must, therefore, be 'backed up' by a second 'duplicate' sling. This will ensure that in the event of failure of the initial sling, there will be a suitable backup to prevent the load falling.

(c) Anchor redundancy

Whilst the above backup system will be sufficient in the case of a single-point anchor, which is unquestionably reliable it will generally be necessary to ensure that failure of a single anchor cannot result in complete failure of the system supporting a load. In order to achieve this, at least two anchor points should be used, configured so as to back up each other. This principle is known as anchor redundancy. (See Figure 2.29.)

It should be noted that secondary anchor points must be at least as strong as the primary anchor point. It is not acceptable to utilise multiple poor anchors in an attempt to create a strong anchor system.

(d) Load sharing between anchors

Where anchors are at different positions with respect to the line of loading, equalisation of the anchor system allows the load to be divided and

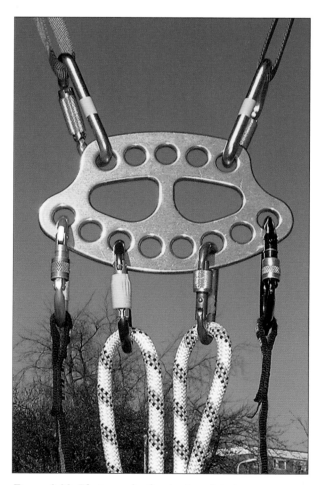

Figure 2.28 Photograph of a rigging plate in use.

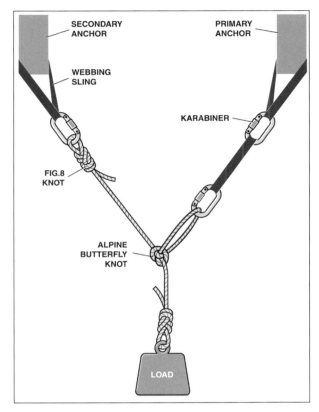

Figure 2.29 Diagram showing one possible configuration of backup system providing anchor redundancy.

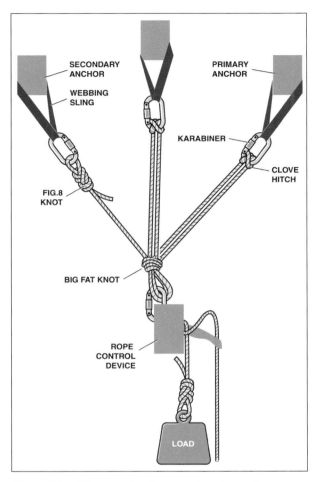

Figure 2.30 Diagram showing a system for anchor equalisation.

distributed between the anchor points. This ensures maximum strength from the available system and also reduces the chance of any individual anchor failing under load. Where any anchor or anchors are not completely reliable, equalisation of the system is essential. Equalisation may be achieved by a number of methods including the use of the Big Fat Knot (BFK). (See Figure 2.30.)

It must be understood that the direction of pull of a load is critically linked to equalisation of anchors and there may be occasions when the load may move to a different angle from its original position. The person having control of ropework operations must try to anticipate any movement of the load and take this into account when setting up the anchor system. This will reduce the risk of any one element of the anchor system being exposed to excessive forces.

(e) Equalising knots and slings
An equalising knot is used to distribute a load between two anchors when it is anticipated that at

some point during the operation, the load will move laterally between the two. To allow this to take place whilst maintaining an even distribution of the load between the two anchors, the load is attached to a single sling by using an equalising knot. Care must be taken when making the knot to ensure that it will remain secure in the event of failure of any one of the anchors. (See Figure 2.31.)

(f) Extension of a system following failure
Where a multiple anchor system is being used, thought has to be given to the effects of one or more of the anchors giving way under load. If such a failure occurs and the equalisation of the anchors has not been correctly applied, there could be an extension of the system towards the load and consequently a shock loading of the remaining anchors. Extension of the system is particularly serious if the belay point is at or near a vertical

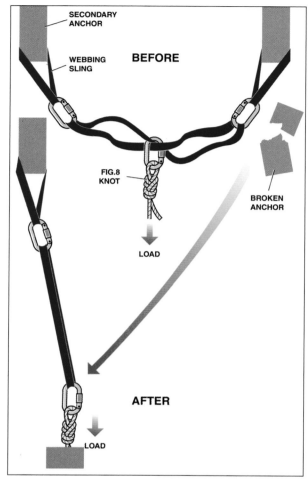

Figure 2.31 Diagram showing the use and failure of a simple equalising system.

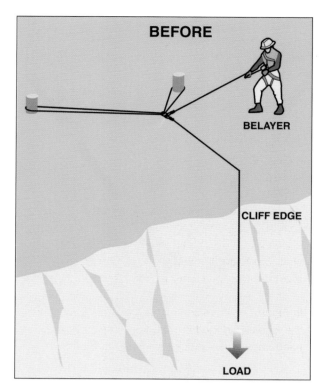

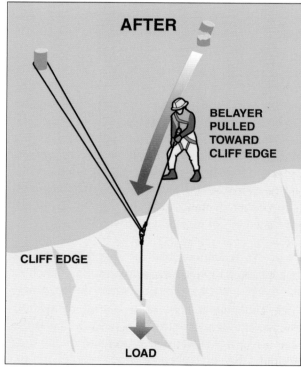

Figure 2.32 Diagrams showing the relocation of the belayer after failure of an anchor.

drop as it could draw the belayer over the edge. (See Figure 2.32.)

(g) Divergence of angles in multiple anchor systems

In anchor systems utilising more than one anchor, the angle that is formed between the anchors and the load will affect the force exerted on each anchor. Some examples and explanations are shown below:

ANCHORS – Angles of Divergence

In the first example (Figure 2.33), an angle is formed between the two legs extending from the anchors at the point where the rope is directed towards the load.

At first glance, it might appear that when a 100kg load is attached to the main system it would be shared evenly between the two anchors, i.e., with each anchor having a loading of 50kg. This is only the case where the angle between the two legs is zero degrees. The actual force on each anchor depends on the angle between the two slings or legs. The wider the angle, the greater the force exerted on each anchor and its associated rigging.

In Figure 2.34, we see that if the angle between the legs is widened to 90 degrees, the forces on each anchor increase significantly to around 71kg.

If the angle is then further widened to 120 degrees (see Figure 2.35) the full weight of the load is exerted onto each of the anchors and its associated rigging. Widening of the angle further still would create stresses on each anchor greater than the load itself.

When dividing loads between anchors angles must, therefore, be kept as low as possible and in any case must not exceed 90 degrees. Reducing the angles and thus reducing the load on each anchor may be achieved by extending the length of the legs from the anchors. Where this is not possible, more anchors should be added to help share the load.

2.3.1.4   Selection of Anchors

When choosing anchors and setting up anchor systems, firefighters must be careful to match the location, size, strength and number of anchors required with the forces that the intended task might place on the system. Whenever possible, individual anchors should be selected so that their maximum strength lies in direct opposition to the loading that will be applied.

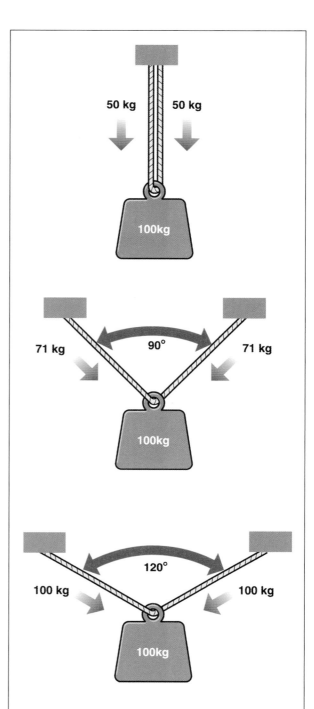

Figure 2.33 (top) Diagram of 2 anchors with weight of 100 kg at an angle of zero degrees. (show individual weight at each anchor as 50Kg)

Figure 2.34 (middle) Diagram of 2 anchors with weight of 100 kg at an angle of 90 degrees. (show individual weight at each anchor as 71Kg)

Figure 2.35 (bottom) Diagram of 2 anchors with weight of 100 kg at an angle of 120 degrees. (show individual weight at each anchor as 100Kg)

In most cases the identification and selection of suitable anchors will be a matter of judgement based on training and experience. In cases of doubt, firefighters should err on the side of safety. It is always better to incorporate too many anchors into a system than too few.

(a) Structural steelwork and masonry

In the absence of purpose built artificial anchors, structural steelwork provides one of the strongest anchors available. Preferred steelwork includes substantial support beams or columns, although welded steel handrails, supports for heavy machinery and large diameter pipes may also be considered. Care should be taken to ensure that:

- The edges of steelwork are effectively protected.
- Handrails are solidly fixed in place.
- Anchors are secured around the base or point of attachment to reduce leverage.
- Pipework is adequately secured and of suitable strength and is neither excessively hot nor cold.
- Insulated pipework should never be used, as the insulation masks the true size and condition of the pipe and could also compress under load, possibly creating a sharp edge that could cut into rope or slings.
- Lightweight or corroded metal and cast iron is avoided.

Where structural steelwork is not available, structural masonry such as reinforced concrete beams or columns may be effectively used. Care should be taken to ensure they are of adequate size and that edges are protected to prevent abrasion.

(b) Ground anchors

Ground anchors may be constructed using round metal bar stakes, 'V' or 'T' section 'angle iron' stakes, or a variety of purpose designed ground plates that can be used either alone or in combination. Stakes should be inserted to their optimum depth and angled away from the anticipated load at approximately 15 to 20 degrees back from the vertical. Tests have shown that when using 'angle iron' as ground stakes, maximum benefit will be achieved by placing the stakes so that the closed edge of the 'V' or the flat edge of the 'T' points towards the load. This will transfer the load to the maximum area of ground contact. (See Figure 2.36.)

When using stakes as ground anchors, especially when working in soft ground where the potential of an individual stake failing is high, it may be necessary to combine a number of stakes to form a single anchor unit. This may be achieved by linking the stakes with slings so that they function as a single unit, commonly known as a 'picket'. Where this is done, the connection between the first and subsequent stakes needs to be as tight as possible in the initial construction of the anchor system. If this is not done, there is a possibility that when the load is applied it will loosen the first stake and render it useless, resulting in a general weakening of the system with the potential to cause progressive collapse of the entire anchor. (See Figure 2.37a.)

Care must be taken to ensure that the load is not allowed to deviate from the direct line of the lead stake, as this will greatly reduce the effectiveness

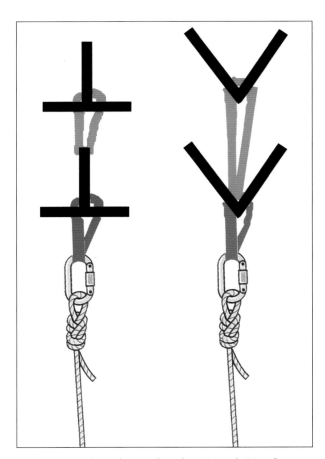

Figure 2.36 Plan of ground anchor 'T' and 'V' stakes.

of the anchor. Where this is likely, the stakes should be arranged in a 'V' configuration to lessen the effect. An alternative method of constructing a combined anchor is by using a metal anchor plate. (See Figure 2.37b.)

(c) Vehicles as anchors

Where no other suitable anchor is readily available, a motor vehicle can be considered for use as an anchor. When using a motor vehicle the following points should be considered:

- The vehicle should be placed on firm level ground.
- The handbrake must be fully applied and the wheels chocked at both front and rear.
- The vehicle should be placed in gear, the ignition keys removed and the vehicle locked.
- If the vehicle cannot be locked, a responsible person must remain in the vicinity to prevent unauthorised interference or movement of the vehicle.

- Particular care must be taken should it be necessary to operate on icy, muddy, waterlogged or sloping ground, as there is a much greater tendency for the vehicle to be moved by the load.
- Structural parts of the vehicle, such as axles and structural cross members should be used as anchors.
- Towing eyes should generally be avoided unless they are of closed construction and are welded or substantially bolted to the chassis.
- Vehicle bumpers, 'bull bars', ladder bars or grab rails should never be used as anchor points.
- Textile items such as rope or webbing slings must not be allowed to come into contact with hot parts of the vehicle such as brake drums, engine or exhaust systems.
- Sharp edges, battery acid, grease and oil must be avoided. Should contamination occur, textile items including ropes may need to be withdrawn from use and destroyed.

Figure 2.37a
Photograph showing angle and orientation of ground stakes.

Figure 2.37b
Photograph showing V-configuration of ground anchor system.

Figure 2.38
Photograph of vehicle being used as a temporary artificial anchor.

Figure 2.39
Photograph of climbing
equipment in use as
temporary artificial
anchor.

(d) Climbing equipment anchors

Temporary anchorages may also be provided by using equipment originally designed for the protection of climbers. These can be positioned in such a way as to act as anchors. Training must be given and personnel assessed to ensure that they are competent in the use of this equipment. Improperly selected or poorly placed equipment could potentially fail with serious consequences.

2.3.1.5 Operational Considerations

To ensure the anchor system is secure, the following points must be considered.

- Individual anchors must be assessed by a competent person as to their suitability for the intended load prior to operations commencing and monitored during use.
- Main anchors should be backed up unless considered 'unquestionably reliable' and the load applied to them limited to an acceptable level.
- Anchors should be protected against mechanical and abrasive damage.
- The angles created by multiple anchors must be monitored and kept as narrow as practicable.
- Before committing load to a vertical environment, all slack should be removed from the ropes.
- Erratic movement on lines or systems must be avoided as this can induce high stress loading on anchors.
- The area around anchors must be kept tidy to allow easy monitoring of the system for any possible movement.

2.4 Securing Casualties, Equipment and Other Items

In operational situations personnel may need to use rope or cord, together with knots and hitches to join or secure items of equipment or other objects. Some tasks are routine and appropriate methods can be pre-planned and practiced. Other tasks are not routine, requiring more on site planning and closer supervision to ensure that they are achieved in a safe and efficient manner.

2.4.1 Knots

Whilst some operational objectives using rope can be achieved by having fixed loops or connectors permanently attached to the end of a rope, on most occasions the operational use of rope or cordage will require the selection and tying of various knots. Appropriate harnesses must always be used to secure firefighters or casualties to a rope. Direct attachment of a rope to a person does not constitute a safe system of work.

2.4.1.1 General

A knot may be defined as the interlacement of cordage in specific patterns for the purpose of stopping ends, joining ends, forming loops and securing equipment. There are a number of standard terms used to describe parts of a knot or rope as follows:

- Bend – to fasten a rope to another rope or to an object.

- Bight – the looped or loose part of a rope between two ends.

- Hitch – a simple fastening of a rope to some object by passing the rope round the object and crossing one part over another.

- Running end – the free end of a rope.

- Running part – the moving part of a rope that is loose and is used to hoist and lower.

- Seizing – the binding together of two or more ropes or parts of one rope to stop them moving in relation to each other.

- Standing Part – the part of a rope that is nearest the eye, bend or hitch, as opposed to the end.

- Whipping – binding of the end of a rope with twine to prevent it unlaying or unravelling.

A knot may be formed with a number of loops, hitches or turns involving one or both ends of a rope or of two different ropes and each knot may be tied in a number of ways using different sequences. There are a number of different knots available, some of which have specific functions, whilst others can be used in a number of situations and for more general applications.

2.4.1.2 Principles of Knot Tying

The general requirements of a knot are:

- It should carry out the function for which it is intended, safely and without slipping.
- It should be easy to tie.
- The knot and its intended use should not damage the rope.
- It should be easy to untie.

All knots will weaken rope. The amount by which this occurs depends principally on how tight the radii of the turns within the knot are. The smaller the radius, the weaker the rope will become at the knot. The amount by which the strength of the rope is reduced may be lessened by using large knots such as a Double Loop Figure 8, or by increasing the amount of rope within the knot such as in a "Big Fat Knot" (BFK), tied in a doubled or quadrupled rope. This not only improves the strength of the rope but will also make the knot easier to untie. To reduce the effect of weakening

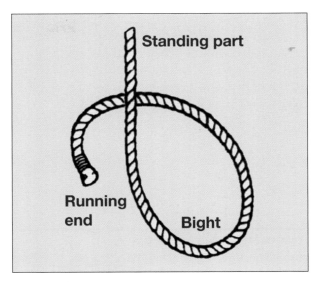

Figure 2.40 Diagram of parts of a rope.

the rope and to make the knot as safe as possible, every knot should be correctly made and tightened.

To maintain the integrity and security of a knot, a 'stopper' knot should be tied in the running end of the rope. Commonly used stopper knots are the Overhand Knot, the Figure 8 Stopper Knot or the Single Fisherman's Knot. In safety-critical applications, the running end should be tied off around the standing part using a suitable knot such as a Double Fisherman's Knot. The tail remaining on the running end of the rope after tying a suitable stopper knot and/or tying off the running end should be at least 100 mm to allow for slippage and ensure that the knot remains secure.

Many knots provide ideal solutions to specific tasks, although their specialist nature may lead to infrequent use. This is often compounded by a complicated tying method leading to difficulty in correctly applying the knot. Consideration should, therefore, be given to keeping the knots in use in brigades as simple and effective as possible. To ensure that the most appropriate knot or knots are selected for a particular application, firefighters must consider the following:

- The purpose of the knot within the ropework system.
- Whether the knot will remain secure in the intended application.
- Whether it will adequately support any intended or anticipated load.

Firefighters must be competent in tying knots in the range of conditions likely to be met in operational situations. They must also be able to adapt knots and lashings to a particular situation and training should prepare personnel for dealing effectively with non-standard tasks.

2.4.1.3   Types of Knot

(a) 'Standard' Knots

The following table contains a list of knots, bends and hitches that are in general use. In the interest of clarity the 'running end' is not drawn to scale length in the diagrams below. It should in practice be at least 100 millimetres long in every case to prevent the knot untying.

Overhand Knot

Primary Function
Sometimes known as a thumb knot. Used as a stopper knot.

Figure of Eight Stopper Knot

Primary Function
Stopper knot tied in a single rope.

Half Hitch

Primary Function
The basis of a number of knots. Used extensively in conjunction with other knots for securing suction, etc.

Double Sheet Bend

Primary Function
A secure method of joining two lines particularly those of unequal thickness.

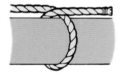

Clove Hitch

Primary Function
Used to secure a line to any round object.

Rolling Hitch

Primary Function
Used to secure a line to any round object so that the knot will not slip along the object when a sideways pull is applied. Often used for securing or hauling hose lines aloft.

Round Turn & Two Half Hitches

Primary Function
Used to secure a line to any round object.

Fisherman's Bend

Primary Function
This is an alternative to the Round Turn & Two Half Hitches that allows the rope to slide up and down or along the beam or spar to which it has been tied.

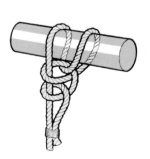

Figure 2.41 Standard Knots.

Bowline

Primary Function
A non-slipping knot also known as the single bowline. Should only be used to secure a person where a purpose made harness or rescue strop is not available.

Running Bowline

Primary Function
A bowline tied around the standing part to form of a running noose.

Figure 2.41 (continued) Standard Knots.

(b) Specialist Knots

There are a number of specialist knots which perform specific functions within rope systems in a variety of environments. They often act on the rope itself to provide frictional resistance e.g. the Italian Hitch or to limit direction of rope travel e.g. the Prusik. They are generally only suitable for use with modern kernmantel ropes or nylon webbing.

The knots described are not an exhaustive list and other knots may be suitable for specific tasks.

Alpine Butterfly Knot

Primary Function
To create a loop in the centre of a rope that can be loaded in any direction.

Double Fisherman's Knot

Primary Function
For joining two ropes together using two opposing barrel stop knots.

Barrel Knot

Primary Function
For tying off a running end.

BFK (Big Fat Knot)

Primary Function
For creating a set of loops from rope or ropes, usually as part of a multi-anchor system.

Figure 2.42 Specialist Knots.

Prusik Knot

Primary Function
Tied with a loop of small diameter accessory cord around a rope to create a locking knot.

Note: A prusik knot does not comply with LOLER unless given a SWL by supplier.

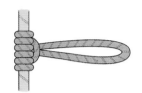

Double Loop Figure 8

Primary Function
For forming two loops using a bight of rope.

Klemheist Knot

Primary Function
Tied with a loop of nylon tape around a rope to create a locking knot.

Note: A Klemheist knot does not comply with LOLER unless given a SWL by supplier.

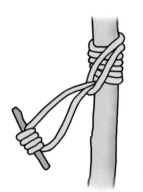

Rethreaded Figure 8 Knot

Primary Function
For tying on directly to a harness or round a fixed object.

Mariner's Knot

Primary Function
Locking off a pulley system. Can be released under load.

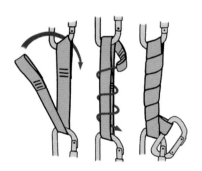

Italian Hitch

Primary Function
Used in conjunction with a karabiner to create frictional resistance to lower a load under control.

Must not be used without additional equipment to create a fail safe system when dealing with live or heavy loads.

Single Loop Figure 8

Primary Function
For forming a single loop.

Tensionless Hitch (or No-Knot)

Primary Function
To provide an anchor without significantly reducing the strength of the rope.

Figure 2.42 (continued) Specialist Knots.

2.4.2 Lifting, Lowering and Hauling

All lifting and lowering operations, from simple hauling aloft of equipment to advanced casualty rescue, fall within the scope of The Lifting Operations and Lifting Equipment Regulations (LOLER). The requirement to comply with Manual Handling Regulations will also have implications for the design of lifting and lowering systems and their operation. Lifting, lowering and hauling systems all require the following principal components.

2.4.2.1 Secure anchors

Any load should be securely attached to a dedicated anchor system, unless:

- It is light weight; and
- A risk assessment confirms it can be safely controlled without a dedicated anchor; and
- There are no safety critical considerations

2.4.2.2 A secure method of attaching the load

When attaching loads for lifting or lowering purposes they must be secured so that they cannot slip or fall, by:

- Enclosing the load in a harness, lifting bag or net, or where this is not possible.
- Securing the load by means of purpose designed strops or slings. otherwise.;
- Tying the load directly on to the rope by use of appropriate knots.

2.4.2.3 A controlled lifting / hauling system

Lifting or hauling operations will either rely on:

- Direct force, such as fire fighters hauling a length of hose aloft. or
- Indirect force, applied through a winch or pulley system.

In both cases the force applied must be sufficient to overcome the force being exerted by a combination of gravity, friction over edges and within the system itself. Lifting lightweight items of equipment may be achieved by simply pulling

on a rope. Heavier loads may require the use of a proprietary winch or pulley system to provide mechanical advantage. When undertaking lifting and hauling operations the following should be considered:

- As hauling systems rely on some degree of mechanical advantage, there is a risk of exceeding the working load limit at the points where the system attaches to the load and to the anchor.
- The risk of the load becoming snagged must not be overlooked. Any tendency to overcome additional resistance by increasing the power input has the potential to injure casualties and rescuers, or overload the system causing it to fail.
- Lifting system should be set up so that once lifting stops an auto-locking device or appropriate knot automatically holds the load at the height to which it has been raised. Once held, there must be a facility to release the load so that it can be lowered again under control.
- Where a lifting or hauling system is used to move a live load, an independent back up system must be deployed to hold the load should the primary system fail.

2.4.2.4 A controlled lowering system

'Lowering' describes any operation that relies on rope to control the distance and rate of descent of a load. Lowering systems use the force of gravity to generate movement, the rate of which is controlled by physically applying friction to the rope through a rope-control device, friction brake or by hand to ensure that the load does not descend in an uncontrolled fashion.

The weight of the load is a critical factor when deciding which system or equipment to use. If the load is lightweight, it may be feasible to either lower hand over hand whilst wearing gloves or control the speed of descent by a turn round a bollard or the use of an Italian Hitch.

As the weight of the load increases however, it becomes more difficult to maintain control by physical strength alone and a rope control device should be used.

Figure 2.43 Photograph of an artificial high directional (AHD) in use at an edge.

The following points should be considered before commencing lowering operations:

- Anchor systems must be of sufficient strength to support the load.
- Ropes must be of sufficient length to reach at least the full distance that the load is to be lowered, unless personnel are competent to pass knots through the system.
- Suitable edge protection is in place.
- A suitable knot (such as a figure 8 stopper knot) is tied near the end of the rope so that it will not pass through the lowering device.
- Lowering devices should be suitable for the load that may be applied.
- Lowering devices should be suitable for the type of load to be lowered (auto-locking devices should be used for live loads).
- There should be a suitable backup system in place where appropriate.
- A hauling system should be available to raise the load should the need arise, e.g. the load becoming snagged during the lower.

- A safe route of egress at the base of the lower should be identified and maintained.

2.4.2.5 Rope & Equipment Protection

Whenever ropes or fabric slings are laid across loose ground, abrasive surfaces or an edge, every effort must be made to ensure adequate precautions are taken to protect the equipment from damage. Points to consider include:

- When exposed to a sharp or abrasive edge, a tensioned rope or sling is more vulnerable to failure than when not under tension.
- Rope protection is especially important with 'non-moving' ropes and slings where the same part is in constant contact with the edge.
- Moving ropes, whilst less vulnerable to damage from edges, are more prone to dislodge rocks and other debris, which may fall onto personnel or equipment.
- The method of protection selected should not hinder the use of the rope or sling.

Figure 2.44 Edge Protection

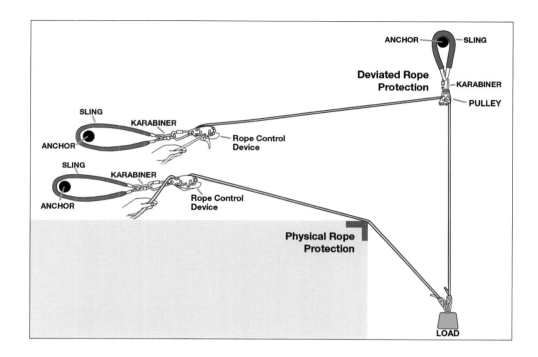

Suitable methods of protection are to:

- Redirect the rope through a pulley at a high point above the edge or hazard. This will prevent the rope from dragging over the edge and will make it easier to load. The pulley can be suspended from a suitable anchor or a metal frame or tripod may be needed to provide the necessary anchor point. It is important to ensure that equipment used in this fashion is suitable for the high forces that can be imposed upon it including an adequate margin for safety above those forces.

- Protect the rope using proprietary equipment such as pads, mats or rollers. Where this is not available improvised protection may be provided using equipment such as salvage sheets, chimney sheets or equipment bags.

Figure 2.45 Photographs of various types of rope edge protection.

2.4.3 Winches and Pulley Systems

2.4.3.1 General

Lifting or hauling lightweight items of equipment may be safely achieved by using rope, with appropriate knots and manual handling techniques. Heavier loads, such as rescuing people or moving heavy objects, will generally require the use of winches or pulley systems.

2.4.3.2 Winching Systems

Winching systems can be either manually operated or powered by some form of electric, hydraulic or fuel-driven power unit. Powered winches offer the advantage of speed in use, a simple system of work and minimum numbers of personnel to operate. They may be difficult to control with sufficient accuracy to safely lift a live load and the potential hazard of a person being caught on an obstacle must be considered. The system must be capable of being stopped quickly if necessary.

Manually operated winches are better suited for the lifting and hauling of people but can be slow in operation. They can be divided into the following groups, dependent upon their method of operation:

- Capstan winches.
- Rope clamp winches.

(See Figure 2.46.)

2.4.3.2 Pulley Systems

A pulley system or 'tackle' is a combination of pulleys through which a rope is threaded in such a way that a force applied to one end is increased. This increase in force is dependent upon the number of pulleys in the system and the manner in which the rope is rove through them. Pulleys containing more than one sheave are known as pulley blocks. The block being the shell or body in which the sheaves are housed.

The pulley blocks in a 'tackle' or pulley system are known as the 'standing block' and the 'moving block'. The standing block is attached to the anchor and the moving block is attached to the load. The rope that is rove through the pulleys is known as the 'fall' and has a 'standing part', a 'hauling part' and a 'running part'. (See Figure 2.47.)

A third type of pulley block is the 'directional block' or 'directional pulley'. The function of the directional pulley is simply to alter the direction of the hauling part of the rope. It does not confer any increase in force to the pulley system itself. Directional pulleys must always be attached to an anchor, never to the load. Any number of directional pulleys may be used in a system to obtain the necessary direction of haul. As with all pulleys, however, there will be some loss of efficiency due to friction within each pulley and the number of directional pulleys should, therefore, be kept to a minimum. (See Figure 2.48.)

Figure 2.46 Photographs of Capstan and Rope Grab Winches.

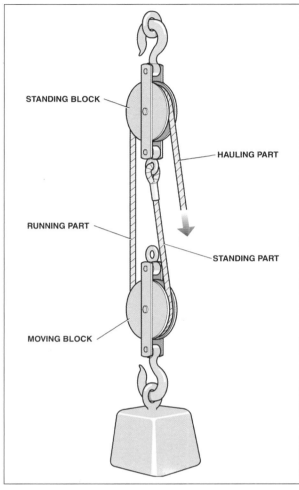

Figure 2.47 Diagram of a pulley system, showing blocks and the rope connecting them.

2.4.4 Mechanical Advantage and Velocity Ratio

Lifting and hauling systems can be configured in a variety of ways but all rely on the concepts of mechanical advantage and velocity ratio to multiply a force exerted on a rope. Thus it is possible for firefighters, either as individuals or in teams, to lift or haul loads that exceed bodyweight.

(a) Mechanical Advantage

The amount by which the force exerted on the hauling part is multiplied by the pulley system is known as the mechanical advantage (MA) and in a simple system, excluding frictional loss, is the same as the number of parts of the rope at the moving block.

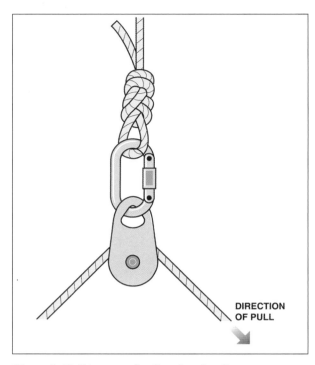

Figure 2.48 Diagram of a directional pulley.

In Figure 2.49 , there are two parts at the moving block, therefore, the mechanical advantage is two (MA = 2). In this situation the force exerted on the hauling part to lift the load of 100 Kg is only 50 Kg.

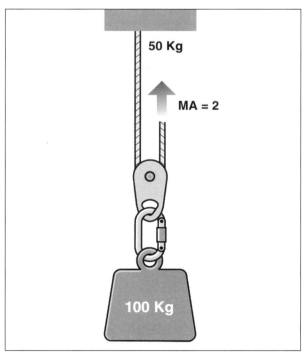

Figure 2.49 Diagram of a simple pulley system with a MA of 2.

(b) Velocity Ratio

Mechanical advantage is only gained at the expense of speed of working. It can be seen that, for any two metres of movement on the hauling part, the load will only be lifted through a distance of one metre. The ratio between the distance moved by the hauling part and the distance moved by the load is known as the 'velocity ratio', referred to as X:1. In a simple system X is always the same as the number of parts of the rope at the moving block.

In any pulley system, considerable friction is created, both in the bearings within each pulley block and by the rope passing over the pulleys. This friction accounts for the difference between the mechanical advantage and the velocity ratio of the pulley system. In a simple system where the velocity ratio is 3 (3:1), friction may reduce the mechanical advantage to about 2.3 (MA = 2.3).

(c) Rove to Advantage/Disadvantage

The number of parts at the moving block and therefore the velocity ratio is always greater when the hauling part comes away from the moving block. A pulley system using this configuration is said to be 'rove to advantage'. In circumstances, usually caused by topography or the need to alter the direction of pull, where the hauling part comes away from the standing block, is said to be 'rove to disadvantage'. (See Figure 2.50.)

2.4.4.1   Simple and Complex Pulley Systems

Pulley systems are extremely adaptable and can be configured in a variety of ways to achieve different functions. Pulley systems can be classified as simple or complex.

(a) Simple Pulley Systems

Simple pulley systems are straightforward to construct and operate and are generally suitable for use by all firefighters. These systems consist of one moving block and one standing block. Each block may have one, two or even three pulleys. They are designed to be quick to set up and easy to use but are usually limited to a mechanical advantage of 2, 3 or 4. Some manufactured systems are pre-rigged using small diameter cord and can create velocity ratios of 6:1 over a short

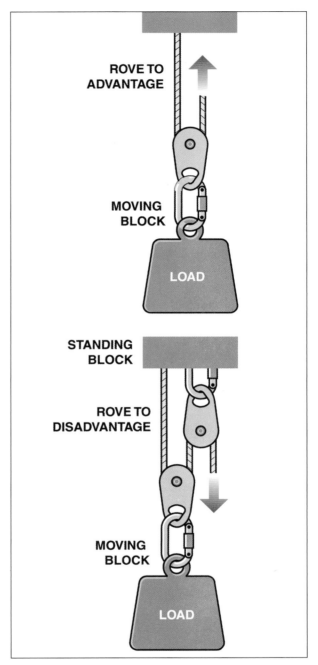

Figure 2.50 Diagrams of a 2:1 pulley system – rove to advantage and rove to disadvantage.

distance. Other pre-rigged systems include a fixed block that also acts as a capstan winch when undertaking lowering operations.

Because each part of the fall extends the full distance between the standing and fixed blocks, simple systems use a lot of rope, e.g. a 3:1 system lifting a load from 10 metres requires in excess of 30 metres of rope. (See Figure 2.51.)

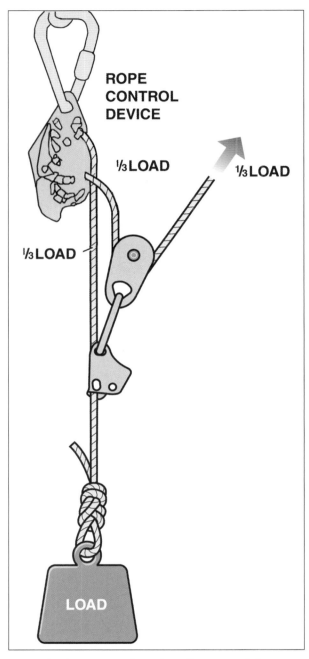

Figure 2.51 Diagram of simple pulley system 3:1.

objects over increased distances. This type of system is essentially a simple pulley system (often 3:1 or 4:1) that instead of being attached directly to the load, is attached to a rope connected to the load, usually by a rope grab. This allows the load to be moved through the full length of a single rope by periodically re-setting the pulley system by operation of the rope grab. (See Figure 2.52.)

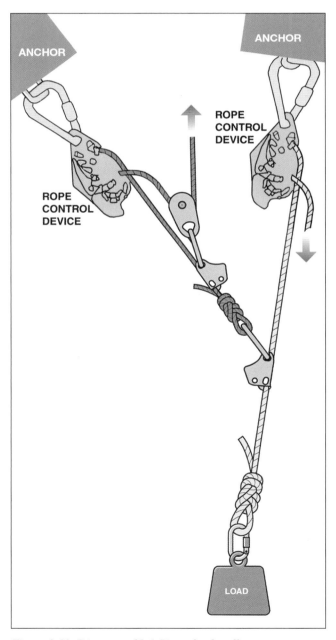

Figure 2.52 Diagram of 3:1 Piggy-back pulley system and rope grab.

(b) Complex Pulley Systems

The nature of complex pulley systems and the high forces they can generate are such that system specific training must be given. Complex systems must be supervised in use and operated by competent personnel. There are two main forms of complex pulley system:

'Piggy-back' Pulley Systems

To overcome the limitations of simple systems, a 'piggy-back' system can be used to lift or haul

Compound Pulley Systems

These systems are constructed by using one pulley system to act directly on a second system, thus multiplying the force that can be exerted on the load. The moving block of the second system is usually attached to the hauling part of the first system by a rope grab. For example, a 3:1 system connected to a 2:1 system will generate a velocity ratio of 6 (6:1). (See Figure 2.53.)

2.4.4.2 Selection of Appropriate Systems

When selecting the appropriate system for a particular operational situation, the degree of mechanical advantage required can be determined from:

- A manual handling assessment.
- The number of competent personnel available.
- The work area that is available, as space may be very limited.
- The effective weight of the load.
- The distance to be travelled by the load.
- The urgency of the situation and the time available to undertake the work.

2.4.4.3 Operational Considerations

When constructing and using pulleys and pulley systems the following points should be considered:

- A dynamic risk assessment encompassing manual handling issues.

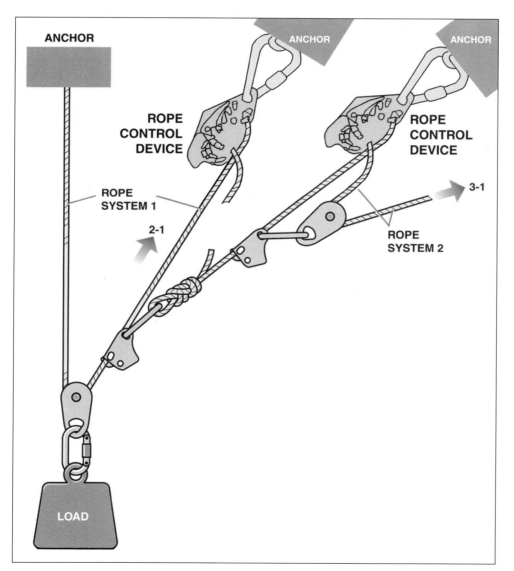

Figure 2.53 Diagram of Compound pulley system.

- The load placed on the anchor of any pulley can be up to twice the load being lifted, therefore anchors for pulley systems must be unquestionably reliable.
- For maximum efficiency in lifting operations, pulley systems should be anchored directly above the working area or a directional pulley should be provided directly above the work area.
- Personnel operating pulley systems in the hazard zone must be provided with the appropriate PPE and linked to a suitable anchor.
- The force exerted over an edge when using a hauling system is greater than the force produced when lowering a load. This increased force can damage ropes and increase abrasion so all edges must be well protected or alternatively, ropes should be deviated away from abrasion points.
- The force applied to a pulley system must be controlled, as it is easy to exceed the safe working limits of equipment when systems that provide mechanical advantage are employed.
- A suitable rope control device should be used in the pulley system to prevent uncontrolled descent of the load should it be necessary to release the hauling part.
- Where the load being hauled or lifted is a person, a separate safety rope system that will prevent the uncontrolled descent of the person in the event of a failure in the pulley system should be employed.
- Effective communications within the team operating the pulley system are vital to ensure safe operation. Signals to pull, stop, release and lower must be clear and pre-determined. Where possible the load should be under close observation throughout the lifting or hauling operation. Hand signals are detailed in Appendix 7 of Fire and Rescue Service Manual Volume 4, 'Fire Service Training, Foundation Training and Development'.
- Firefighters pulling on the hauling part of a pulley system must stop as soon as any increase in resistance is felt as this may indicate the load has jammed. Continued strain on the hauling part can quickly lead to dangerous forces being created or, if the load is a person, to serious injury.

2.4.5 Securing Casualties and Performing Rescues from Height

When deciding appropriate equipment and systems to use for the rescue of casualties, the determining factors will be:

- Physical environment.
- Casualty's injuries.
- Medical requirements.
- Time constraints.
- Available resources.

If the casualty's condition or situation requires immediate rescue the use of work at height equipment may not be appropriate. The decision to undertake a rescue from height without work at height equipment can only be taken after a robust dynamic risk assessment. This type of rescue could include assisted ladder walk-downs and casualty carrydown.

Other than the most urgent of rescues, any system used should allow for basic first aid procedures to be applied throughout the rescue and facilitate any medical interventions or care required by the casualty. It is often more effective to limit medical care to basic life saving measures and evacuate quickly in order to begin advanced medical treatment on more secure terrain where the casualty is more accessible to qualified medical personnel and equipment.

In order to offer medical, physical and emotional support it may be necessary for the casualty to be accompanied by a rescuer throughout the evacuation. In rope-based systems, this approach will increase the loading on the anchors and the equipment and therefore specific consideration must be taken of the forces applied to the components within the system.

When it is not feasible to raise a combined load consideration should be given to raising the casualty and rescuer individually.

2.4.5.1 Securing Casualties

Immediately upon accessing the casualty, an assessment of the situation must be made to determine whether immediate evacuation is required and what equipment and systems of work can be implemented.

If immediate evacuation is not necessary then casualties should be secured against the risk of falling, until suitable systems of work can be implemented.

The casualty should not be directly attached to a rope unless there is an immediate risk of the casualty falling and a proprietary rescue sling or harness is unavailable.

2.4.5.2   Rescue

There is a hierarchy that should be applied when deciding the method of rescuing casualties from height. This will be determined by the circumstances of each incident and risk assessments must give due consideration to the following options:

●   Remove casualties to a place of safety via a safe route or existing means of egress, such as an internal stairway, which doesn't require any additional safety equipment.

●   If time and circumstances permit an aerial appliance may be appropriate. Specific considerations include:
    ■   Availability.
    ■   Access.
    ■   Overhead hazards.
    ■   Underground hazards.
    ■   Increased rescue loads.
    ■   Time constraints.
    ■   Operating envelope.

●   In situations where neither of these options are viable or reasonable then the use of rope based systems may be appropriate. Rope systems for casualty rescue should incorporate the following:
    ■   A casualty harness, rescue strop or stretcher.
    ■   Two independent rope systems.
    ■   A secure anchor point for each rope system.
    ■   Two rope control devices; one to control the rate of descent, one to provide a backup in the event of failure.

Figure 2.54 Diagram of fire fighters carrying out casualty evacuation using two rope system and rope control devices attached to an improvised anchor.

For simplicity, back up system not shown.

When using rope systems, the route by which the casualty is to be rescued and the method of movement should be established before starting work. If a casualty is stranded at height the most suitable route may be to lower them, providing egress is available from the base of the hazard zone. Raising and traversing with casualties is more complex and places greater requirements on resources and higher loadings on equipment.

● If immediate rescue is necessary to prevent serious injury or death, the most appropriate solution may be to use fire and rescue service ladders for assisted walk-downs or carry-downs. (See Figure 2.55.)

2.4.6 Casualty Management

2.4.6.1 Suspension Trauma (Orthostatic Intolerance)

With the increasing use of harnesses and rope systems for recreation and in the workplace, a medical condition associated with prolonged suspension has been identified. Known as orthostatic intolerance or suspension trauma, the condition occurs where an immobile person is suspended in a harness or from a rope system. A prolonged period of suspension can result in serious trauma in less than 30 minutes whether or not a harness is worn.

In unconscious, immobile and injured casualties suspension trauma has been known to be fatal in as little as 2 to 3 minutes. Factors that may affect casualties in suspension and lead to orthostatic shock include:

● Exhaustion.
● Hypothermia.
● Hypoglycaemia.
● Head trauma.
● Dehydration.
● Shock.
● The degree of inclination of the body.
● Time delay in casualty access.

If possible, movement of the casualty's limbs whilst suspended may mitigate the effects of orthostatic shock; however, rapid evacuation from the suspended position to immediate medical treatment is the preferred option. The possibility of suspension trauma must always be considered with any suspended casualty. However, the casualty's other injuries must not be ignored.

Figure 2.55 The relationship between risk, time available and the selection of rescue method.

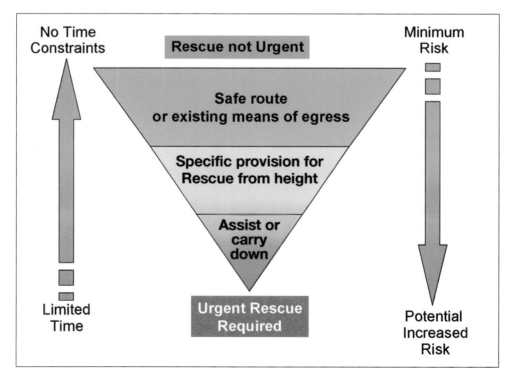

2.4.6.2   Stretcher Rescues

Casualties whose condition or injuries do not allow for the use of casualty harnesses during rescue may need to be packaged and removed using a stretcher. Generally, unconscious casualties and those with major or spinal injuries should always be transported by stretcher in a horizontal position, with movement in a vertical position only being temporarily used to negotiate obstacles. When using stretchers the following points must be addressed:

- The stretcher and associated equipment must be fit for the intended use.
- The stretcher and associated equipment must be used within a safe system of work at all times (e.g. during the transfer at height of the stretcher to an aerial appliance).
- Extra loading on the system due to the use of operators as stretcher attendants.
- Physical protection for the casualty to prevent injury.
- Warm clothing or covering for the casualty to prevent hypothermia.

The use of attendants accompanying stretchers in rope rescue should be considered an advanced technique and fire and rescue services will wish to restrict such stretcher use to specialist teams. There are many systems of work suitable for use with stretchers and further advice can be sought from the National Rope Users Group or specialist training providers.

2.5   Operational Environments

2.5.1   Existing Places of Work

An 'existing place of work' at height is best thought of as a place of work with permanent fall prevention measures such as guard rails or a parapet and no need for any additional equipment to remove the risk of a fall. Parts of buildings or permanent structures (including the means of access and egress) generally fall into this category and should be used for work at height in preference to any place provided by temporary work equipment.

An existing (safe) place of work can change, due to changing conditions, for example:

- The structure may become unstable due to fire spread, etc.
- If windows are removed or broken and as a result unprotected openings are created.

Any change in circumstances that give rise to the risk of a potential fall means that a location can no longer be considered an 'existing' place of work. Dynamic risk assessment must be undertaken and the situation monitored at regular intervals, with appropriate actions taken to prevent a fall or mitigate the consequences.

Some examples of an existing place of work that can be considered 'safe' are:

- A non-fragile roof with a permanent parapet or guard rail.
- A silo or storage tank etc, with fixed guardrails.
- Mezzanine floor with fixed edge protection.

Additionally, safe places of work at height should:

- Be stable and of sufficient strength and stability.
- Be of sufficient dimension to allow safe work and passage of persons and materials.
- Have suitable and sufficient means of preventing a fall.
- Not present slip, trip & fall hazards.
- Have no surface gap through which a person could fall.

A drill tower may be considered a 'safe place of work' if the risk assessment considers that all of the above apply e.g. the internal ladder access gap will need to be adequately protected and the top of railings or parapets on roofs and window openings are of adequate height to prevent a fall.

2.5.2   Unprotected Edges

Unprotected edges, where there is a risk of a fall, may be found in a range of work environments, including:

- Roofs.
- Cliffs and Embankments.
- Shafts, wells, sewers, etc.
- Railway rolling stock, large goods vehicles, buses, aircraft, etc.
- Shipping.
- Silos, storage tanks, industrial plant, etc.

The normal hierarchy for work at height applies in all these environments, irrespective of whether they are stable, in normal condition, or have been damaged by some sort of incident.

The height of edge protection and other appropriate control measures to prevent falls from these environments should be derived through an appropriate risk assessment. This must consider the range of people who may be at risk (including children), with the height of barriers and any gaps in them being such that accidental falls are prevented. It can be seen, therefore, that there is no defined universal height for barriers that provide collective protection from falls.

A minimum barrier height of 950mm is defined in Schedule 2 of the Regulations. This requirement only applies to work at height during construction work covered by the Construction (Health, Safety and Welfare) Regulations 1996. It may, however, be used as a good practice guide in other environments although the actual height required must be determined through a risk assessment as relevant to each particular circumstance.

Where edge protection is not present, and construction of such protection is not feasible within available timescales, such as during the early stages of emergency work, then risk can be avoided by preventing access to the hazard zone. Based on the maximum distance that an individual could conceivably slip or trip, on level ground, this should extend a minimum of 3 metres from any:

- Unguarded edge.
- Sloping surfaces or embankment leading to an unguarded edge.

Figure 2.56 Example of edge protection retrofitted to a flat roof to prevent falls from height.

As an incident progresses supervision by a safety officer and the erection of simple barriers, such as tape or rope will identify the safe work area and access routes to it. Small openings may be protected by securing props horizontally across the opening.

2.5.3 Roofs – Flat Roofs, Sloping Roofs and Fragile Roofs

The risks of working on roofs are substantial however long or short the work and high standards of safety are necessary at all times. The principal risks are falls through fragile roofing materials and falls from unprotected roof edges. The normal hierarchy applies, with the first control measure being to avoid working on roofs. Where avoidance is not possible, a risk assessment should be carried out and a safe system of work adopted, for example eliminating or reducing the distance of any fall by:

- Working from an 'existing place of work'.
- Utilising an aerial appliance.

Getting on and off a roof is a major risk in itself. A secure means of access/egress is essential. Ladders are commonly used, although access may be gained by use of an aerial platform or via internal stairways. Aerial platforms provide a safe workplace and should always be considered as an alternative to working on the roof itself or off a ladder.

Many other methods of accessing roofs may be available to fire and rescue service personnel at an incident, including scaffolding, MEWPS, suspended access equipment, masts and platforms. Before any such method of access is used a full risk assessment must be carried out with advice taken from appropriate competent persons, as the history of erection, use and maintenance may not be available to fire and rescue service staff.

The Regulations do not prohibit working on a roof from a ladder, but ladders must be used appropriately after a risk assessment has been carried out.
It should be noted that not all roof construction systems can support the weight of a person under normal conditions and generally stable strong roof structures can be significantly weakened by fire or collapse. In cases of doubt, a roof structure should be considered fragile and appropriate precautions taken.

2.5.3.1   Hierarchy of Control

Avoid
It is important that personnel planning for, or responding to incidents involving roof work, make a conscious effort to identify alternative methods of work such as working from the ground, an aerial appliance or staging. As an example, attacking a chimney fire from the grate is usually the simplest and quickest method. It avoids the need to carry equipment aloft and work at height thereby eliminating the risk of falls and of anything falling onto someone below.

Prevent
Where working on a roof cannot be avoided, prevent the risk of a fall by using available protection such as guardrails and travel restraint systems. Where prevention is impracticable, reduce the risk by using roof ladders, roof platforms, crawl boards and similar equipment.

Mitigate
Where the risk of a fall from a roof can't be avoided, suitable collective protection or personal protection systems must be used.

2.5.4 Flat Roofs

Falls from flat roofs not only occur from the edges, but also through openings or gaps in the roof and through fragile roof material.

Before walking or working on a flat roof, it is important to identify its strength and stability. Flat roofs can often be used for working on e.g. installation or maintenance of ventilation equipment etc, but some are fragile and may not have the ability to support the weight of a person and are not designed for walking or working on.

2.5.5 Sloping Roofs

For safety assessments it is not practical to determine the specific angle which distinguishes sloping roofs from flat roofs. Falls are most likely if the slope is steep, if the surface is slippery and in windy conditions. Different materials of construction and environmental variables, such as moisture, ice, snow and lichens all influence the degree of risk. Key considerations when working with sloping roofs are:

- The roof surface should not be directly stepped on unless suitable protection from a fall is in place.
- The slope can obscure the view of the ground giving a false sense of height and security.
- It may be difficult to arrange secure anchors for personal protection systems.

Falls from sloping roofs are a common cause of serious accidents and most frequently occur when working at the eaves or gable ends, by slipping on the exterior surface or by breaking through into the interior void.

Edge protection should be put in place for work on sloping roofs unless the work is of short duration. Emergency fire and rescue service work will generally fall into the short duration category, for which the erection of edge protection may be impractical. Safe systems of work must, however, provide:

- Safe means of access to roof level.
- A properly constructed and securely pitched roof ladder.

Roof ladder anchorage should bear on the opposite roof and not depend on the roof ridge capping as this can break away. Roof ladders rely on load being applied at right angles to the surface on which they rest, to ensure that the securing hook at the head of the ladder, and the bearers under the ladder, transfer load to the roof structure evenly across their entire surface. Any twisting or turning movement may jeopardise this security. Consequently, roof ladders should only be considered as secure anchorage for work restraint or fall arrest systems after dynamic risk assessment. Where they are to be used as a work location for anything more than short duration operations, an independent fall protection system, using an alternative anchorage, is preferable. This can be achieved by deploying fall protection systems anchored at ground level on the opposite side of the building, with securing lines passing up over the roof, to firefighters working on the other side of the premises.

Subject to a suitable risk assessment, it may be safe to work without a roof ladder when the pitch of a sloping roof is shallow, the surface provides a good foothold and secure edge protection or other appropriate fall protection is provided.

2.5.6 Fragile Roofs/Surfaces

A fragile surface is one that will not support the weight of a person and the load they are carrying. Falls through fragile roofs or surfaces have been identified by the HSE as causing an average of ten fatal accidents per year. Typical examples of fragile roof materials are:

- Plastic/Perspex roof light sheets.
- Fibre cement sheets.
- Corroded metal sheets.
- Glass.
- Wood wool slabs.
- Fire damaged materials.
- Materials weakened by structural collapse. (See Figure 2.57.)

The stability of a surface must be determined before work begins. It can be difficult to distinguish between roof light sheets and metal sheets particularly in certain light conditions and this has been a major factor in past fatal accidents. All roofing sheets should be treated as fragile and should not be directly walked on unless it can be determined absolutely that they are of adequate strength to support the load. Work must be arranged to ensure that personnel do not walk on or work near fragile surfaces. An identified three metre exclusion zone would be appropriate for safe working. General principles are:

ALWAYS:
- Treat Asbestos cement roof or roofs treated with bitumen or any other surface coating as fragile.

DON'T:
- Stand on, walk on or step across any roof-lights.
- Run on or jump onto roof surfaces.
- Drop equipment onto roof surfaces.
- Treat bolt lines as a safe route.

Figure 2.57 Complex roof area with examples of roof lights, fragile surfaces and barriers providing collective protection.

CONSIDER:

- Old roofs treated with bitumen paint/mastic will have many hidden dangers.
- Cracked sheets that will certainly be fragile
- The presence of profiled roof-lights that blend into their surroundings.
- Failing washers and fixings making the roof fragile.

Fragile material should be clearly marked with a sign as indicated on Figure 2.58.

The Regulations provide an exemption for the emergency services from the requirement to use warning signs for fragile surfaces, when acting in an emergency. In an operational environment, if it is not reasonably practicable to provide signage to alert personnel to the presence of fragile surfaces, other measures should be taken such as briefing crews, posting a safety officer or taping an area off. The absence of a warning sign must not be taken to mean the surface is safe and advice should be sought from the premises owner, occupier or other knowledgeable source as to the integrity of the roof.

Some roof coverings can give a false sense of security by supporting an evenly distributed load

Figure 2.58 Typical fragile material warning sign.

but they may not be capable of supporting a concentrated load similar to a person walking over it. The whole of a roof structure needs to be considered, including the overall construction, internal structure, loading, surface, skylights or other openings and weakening due to fire or structural damage.

Key points for roof work:

- Avoid roof work where possible.
- Use work equipment or other measures to prevent falls.
- Where roof work cannot be avoided and the risk of a fall cannot be eliminated, use work equipment or other measures to minimise the distance and consequences of a fall should one occur.

- Ensure safe access and egress from the roof.
- Short duration work where possible.
- Beware of fragile and slippery surfaces.
- Use the most appropriate equipment for the work.
- Control the risks from falling objects when working on a roof.

2.5.7 FRS Vehicles

Working on the decks or roofs of fire and rescue service vehicles should be avoided. Where this is not possible suitable systems of work must be established to prevent falls or mitigate their effects. A range of general principles should be considered and applied as appropriate to local circumstances, including:

Figure 2.59 Access steps and working platform for vehicle maintenance.

- Ensuring that procedures are in place for safe working on the decks and designated access areas or roofs of fire and rescue service appliances. Procedures must include risk assessment and appropriate control measures, specific training requirements, fault reporting and the safe system of work.

- Information and instruction must be provided in relation to both operational and maintenance activities.

- Specifications for new appliances should follow the principle of design that avoids the need for access to parts of the vehicle where there is a risk of a fall, otherwise collective fall prevention measures should be provided. For example, operator control positions could be at ground level by utilising remote control systems. Existing appliances should be reviewed in relation to the same criteria.

- Where collective protection measures are not practicable individual protection may be required, but attention must be given to training and supervision.

- Operator positions on a vehicle must be designed to prevent accidental falls.

- Deck surfaces should be slip resistant and a maintained as such. Trip hazards must be removed, or where this is impractical identified with high visibility markings.

- Deck edge markings and safety signs should be high visibility.

2.5.8 Service and Utility Structures

Structures of this type include masts, pylons, cranes, towers, chimneys, radio/TV aerials, steeples, wind generators, turbines and various other open structures. These structures will often be very high as well as being built in isolated and exposed locations, with safe access requiring technical rope working skills.

The hazards of working on service and utility structures alter significantly according to the type and location of the structure. Specific considerations include:

- Exposed and isolated locations where the effects of the weather and in particular the wind can be extreme and temperatures reduce with increased height. Personnel exposed to these conditions may suffer an early onset of fatigue and exposure.

- Accessing many structures of this type may need lead-climbing techniques to be applied. These require specialist skills, including a comprehensive understanding of fall factors, the use of dynamic ropes and placement of running belay points.

- Working on these types of structure may involve operating at extreme height. The effects of this can include fatigue from the effort of sustained climbing, vertigo caused by the high and exposed location in which activities may have to take place and motion sickness due to the flex and movement of some structures.

- The open nature of structures, such as high masts and tower cranes may lead to some individuals suffering an adverse psychological reaction. This generally relates to the extreme exposure experienced and may not manifest itself in other high environments, such as working on cliffs. Before working on such open structures operationally, personnel should have experienced the level of exposure during training.

- High voltage electricity may be present, particularly on pylons, wind generators and turbines. Such equipment should wherever possible be isolated and earthed before work starts.

- Various types of radio frequency, microwave, infrared, laser or high power light transmission may frequently be present. Such equipment should wherever possible be isolated before work starts in accordance with agreed preplanning.

- Personnel should avoid passing in front of or working in close proximity to transmitters.

- Radio transmission masts, particularly mobile phone masts, may be disguised for environmental reasons and therefore not easily identifiable. Examples include trees, church towers, flagpoles and water towers.

- Machinery with hazardous moving parts may be present, including lifts, winches, hoists and transmission dishes that may move without warning due to remote operation.

- The hazard zone below very high structures may need to be significantly extended as anything falling from high levels may land some distance away from the structure.

- Effective communication can be difficult due to wind noise.
- Voice operated communications equipment may be needed to allow hands-free operation.
- Structure operating companies may have an in-house rescue capability, with specific knowledge relating to the risk, although their response times can be extended. Pre-planning should include liaison with these teams wherever possible.

2.5.9 Trees

Incidents involving rescue from trees may occur in locations with difficult access needing off road vehicles to transport personnel and equipment. Specific points to consider include:

- Specialist tree climbing or lead climbing involving technical rope work skills may be required.
- Anchor selection can be difficult and any branches used as anchors must be thoroughly inspected prior to use.
- Chain saws and other tools that were being used by a casualty may pose additional hazards.
- Advice and assistance that may be available from skilled arboriculture staff on site.
- Casualty rescue may require branches and foliage to be cut to establish a safe rescue route.

2.5.10 Collapsed Structures

When working in or on collapsed structures additional hazards may be encountered due to confined spaces, unprotected edges, unstable ground and surfaces that can cause damage to equipment. It is important to ensure that any work at height equipment is sufficiently robust to operate in these environments and is closely monitored and protected during use to avoid damage that may increase the risk of equipment failure. Consideration must also be given to the requirement for safe work at height practices to be applied as a consequence of the Confined Space Regulations, which may be applicable to some aspects of work in collapsed structures.

When working in or on collapsed structures and there is a risk of a fall from height, the normal hierarchy of control should be used:

- **Avoid:** Is it possible to achieve the task in a different way that does not represent as significant a hazard? As an example USAR crews may be able to utilise an aerial appliance or crane for access to a work site rather than climbing over a rubble pile to gain access.

- **Prevent:** Where there is potential for a fall, work restraint systems may provide a suitable control system, capable of preventing any fall.

- **Mitigate:** Fall arrest and suitable rescue/recovery systems should be available when necessary to reduce the effects of any fall and/or recover any casualties.

At large structural collapse incidents, fire and rescue services and other supporting agencies will often be drawn from a large area and work in close proximity to each other. Compatibility of equipment and procedures must be considered when planning work on a collaborative basis.

2.5.11 Working Near Water

When working at height above or near water, protection from falls must be provided in the same way as in all other work at height environments. Many of the skills and much of the equipment required for technical work at height and water rescue are similar, so in reality the two capabilities are complementary and may be combined.

Compatibility of equipment and procedures must be confirmed when designing dual purpose work at height and water rescue systems. For example, work at height systems are normally designed so that they can not be disconnected under load, but a critical requirement of water rescue systems is that any rescuer entering water must be secured by a system that can be released one-handed by the wearer, whilst under load.

2.5.11.1 Hierarchy of Control

Application of normal risk management systems to work at height near water provides a template for developing control measures:

- **Avoid:** It is important that personnel planning for, or responding to incidents, first consider alternative methods of work. For example, a casualty trapped by the tide at the base of a cliff may be safely rescued by inshore lifeboat rather than by rope up the cliff face.

- **Prevent:** The three metre hazard zone should be observed as a minimum safe distance when there is a risk of a fall into water.

  Where there is the potential for a fall into water when working at height, work restraint or work positioning may provide a suitable control measure. For example a pump operator working on a dockside can be provided with a safe system of work by using work restraint equipment that prevents reaching the unguarded edge.

- **Mitigate:** Where the risk of a fall can not be prevented, appropriate fall arrest systems must be provided to mitigate the effect of a fall and wherever possible prevent accidental entry into water. If circumstances are such that accidental entry into water cannot be ruled out life jackets must be provided and a safety boat utilised as appropriate. Further guidance is provided in Fire Service Manual "Safe Working Near, On or In Water".

2.5.11.2 Ships

Normal shipboard activities carried out solely by the ships' crew, under the direction of the master, are outside the scope of the Regulations. This exemption does not apply to fire and rescue service personnel, who will need to comply with the Regulations when operating on a ship.

2.5.12 Confined Spaces

Working in confined spaces may involve using vertical access or egress routes where personnel can be at risk from a fall. In many circumstances the techniques used to provide safe work at height can be applied, although some specific issues must be considered, including:

- Harnesses and associated equipment must be compatible for use in conjunction with breathing apparatus.
- There is a potential for damage from chemical contaminants and sharp edges to textile based equipment, including ropes and wire rope may be more appropriate.
- Points of access or egress may also be at height and have little or no working platform around them. Aerial appliance cage/platforms or tripod systems above point of entry may be needed to provide high anchor points.
- An emergency or secondary retrieval system must be available throughout any confined space entry.

Chapter 3 – Equipment

3.1 Selection of Equipment

Selection of work equipment and PPE should be based on the requirements of individual FRSs following risk assessment of work environments in line with the requirements of their IRMP.

The range of equipment that should be considered for work at height includes:

- Ladders.
- Aerial appliances.
- Working platforms.
- Scaffolding.
- Ropes, harnesses and associated equipment.

Equipment should be purchased or specified by a competent person who should consider conformity with current standards as part of the selection process. Personal protective equipment meeting the requirements of the European Standards body and showing the 'CE' mark should be selected where possible, although 'non-CE' equipment may be selected where it can be shown as suitable for the intended purpose. 'Certificates of Conformity' should be requested where appropriate. Demonstrations in the correct wearing of PPE must be undertaken as appropriate and at suitable intervals.

Instructions and guidance for use provided by the suppliers of equipment for work at height must always be considered when developing safe systems of work. Suppliers' instructions should be followed whenever they differ from the general guidance given in this document.

3.2 Ladders and Aerial Appliances

3.2.1 Portable Ladders for Fire Service Use

New ladders being procured for introduction into the service should meet the requirements of The Provision and Use of Work Equipment Regulations 1998 and BS EN 1147:2001, portable ladders for fire service use. This standard specifies requirements, test methods and performance criteria for portable ladders for fire service use and associated purposes.

These ladders vary in length and are usually manufactured from aluminium using a riveted and trussed construction. Double or triple extensions are common and the numbers of firefighters needed to pitch them will vary up to a crew of four.

3.2.1.1 Terminology

Firefighters should first ensure they are familiar with the proper terms for the various parts of a ladder as indicated in Figure 3.1. They should note in particular that the fire and rescue service always refers to the rungs of a ladder as the rounds. Firefighters should also familiarise themselves with the following terms used in operations with these ladders:

Extend
> to raise the extending portion, increasing the length of a ladder

Extend to lower
> to raise the extending portion of a ladder to clear the pawls for lowering

Heel in, out

to move the heel of a ladder towards or away from a building

Head in, out

to place the head of the ladder against or move it away from the building

Lower

to retract the extending portion of a ladder

Pitch

to erect a ladder against a building

Slip

to remove a ladder from an appliance

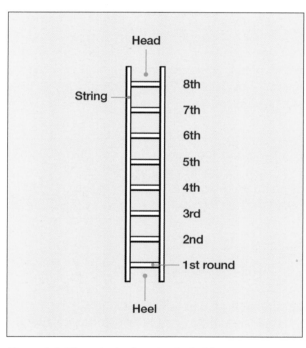

Figure 3.1 The principal parts of a ladder.

3.2.2   Turntable Ladders (TL)

In essence, a turntable ladder is a self-supporting and power-operated extension ladder mounted on a turntable. The ladder assembly is mounted at the rear of a heavy, self-propelled, chassis approximately above the back axle. The ladder itself usually consists of a main ladder, secured by a strong pivot bearing to the swinging frame, and three or four extensions which extend telescopically.

3.2.2.1   Terminology

Firefighters can carry out a number of different manoeuvres with a TL and use it for a variety of purposes. To avoid any confusion the Fire and Rescue Service has adopted a standard terminology for use when referring to the various operations.

Depress

to lower the head of the ladder by reducing the angle of elevation

Elevate

to raise the head of the ladder by increasing the angle of elevation

Extend

to increase the length of the ladder

House

to reduce the length of the ladder

Plumb
(to right or left)

to keep the centre line of the ladder in a vertical plane by eliminating any tilt to one side when the ladder is extended on a slope. This increases stability and obviates side stress

Projection

the horizontal distance measured from a vertical line dropped from the head of the ladder to the rim of the turntable

Shoot up

to extend the ladder with a firefighter already at its head

Train
(to right or left)

to move the head of a ladder by rotating the turntable. (NB manufacturers tend to use the expression 'slewing')

Firefighters should first familiarise themselves with these basic terms and with the various parts of a TL named in Figure 3.2.

3.2.3   Hydraulic Platforms (HP)

Hydraulic platforms consist essentially of two or three booms hinged together. The two lower booms pivot in a vertical plane on each other and on the fulcrum frame, on which the bottom boom is

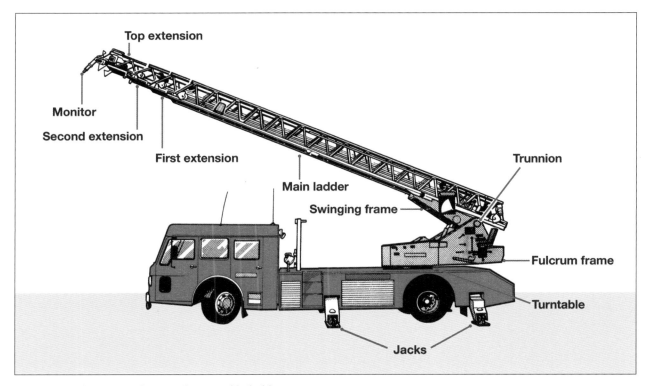

Figure 3.2 The principal parts of a turntable ladder.

hinged. The third boom takes the form of a pivoted or telescopic extension arm at the upper end of the second.

3.2.3.1   Terminology

As with turntable ladders, firefighters have adopted a standard terminology for use when operating HPs.

Booms
> the two or three jointed sections which carry the cage.

Cage
(or platform)
> the personnel compartment at the end of the second or, if fitted, third boom.

Depress
> to reduce the height of the cage.

Elevate
> to increase the height of the cage.

Height
> the distance of the cage bottom from the ground.

Knuckle
> the pivoting joint between booms.

Over-ride
> a control as the base operator's position.

Plumbing
> use of the jacks to compensate for any camber up to five degrees and bring the vehicle level.

Projection
> the distance from the outside of the jack foot to the outside edge of the cage when the bottom boom is fully elevated and the second boom horizontal, at right angles across the chassis.

Safe working load (S.W.L.)
> the specific payload which an HP can normally carry anywhere within its working range. It can be affected by the vehicle being incorrectly plumbed, strong winds, or the imposition of extra loads on the booms, e.g. by use of the monitor.

Train

to move the cage in a circular route by moving the turntable.

Turntable

the revolving platform, exactly on the centre line of the chassis, which carries the fulcrum frame and one end of the bottom boom.

3.2.4 Aerial Ladder Platforms (ALP)

These appliances combine the principal features of the Turntable Ladder and Hydraulic Platforms into one appliance. They usually consist of 2 hydraulically operated telescopic booms and a large rescue cage. Attached to the booms is a large extending ladder, which can be used for access, egress and rescue purposes.

3.2.4.1 Terminology

Extend

to increase the length of the ladder/booms

House

to reduce the length of the ladder/booms

Train
(to right or left)

to move the cage/head of a ladder/booms by rotating the turntable. (NB manufacturers tend to use the expression 'slewing')

Ladder/Booms

the telescopic ladder and booms which carry the cage.

Cage
(or platform)

the personnel compartment at the end of the ladder/booms.

Depress

to reduce the height of the cage.

Elevate

to increase the height of the cage.

Height

the distance of the cage bottom from the ground.

Over-ride

a control as the base operator's position.

Plumbing

use of the jacks to compensate for any camber up to five degrees and bring the vehicle level.

Projection

the distance from the outside of the jack foot to the outside edge of the cage when the ladder/boom is fully elevated and the second boom horizontal, at right angles across the chassis.

Safe working load (S.W.L.)

the specific payload which an ALP can normally carry anywhere within its working range. It can be affected by the vehicle being incorrectly plumbed, strong winds, or the imposition of extra loads on the booms, e.g. by use of the monitor.

Turntable

the revolving platform, exactly on the centre line of the chassis, which carries the fulcrum frame and one end of the bottom ladder/boom.

3.3 Working Platforms

A working platform is any platform used as a place of work, a means of access to, or egress from a place of work at height and includes an aerial appliance fitted with a cage. It also includes any place of work on a scaffold, cradle, mobile platform, trestle, gangway, gantry or stairway. All working platforms should be properly supported and provided with guard-rails and barriers set at the appropriate height. Working platforms must be:

- Of sufficient dimensions to allow safe passage and safe use of equipment and materials.
- Free of hazards that could cause trips, or allow people's feet to pass through the flooring.
- Constructed to prevent feet and objects passing over the edge i.e. toe boards or edge protection are in place.
- Kept clean and tidy e.g. do not allow mud to build up on platforms.
- Secure.

The supporting structure for any working platform must be prevented from moving during work at height and be stable while being erected, used and dismantled.

The surface of any working platform must not have any gap through which a person could fall or through which any item could fall and cause injury. It should also be positioned so that there is no risk of slipping, tripping or any person being caught between the working platform and any adjacent structure.

3.4 Textile Based Equipment

3.4.1 General

Textiles currently in use are generally based on polyamide, polyester webbing, and cordura sheet or nylon derivatives. Webbing tape is generally constructed from nylon thread woven into a web, the longitudinal threads called the warp and the lateral threads called the weft. Webbing tape is light, has great tensile strength and as such forms the core of many types of textile based rope equipment including slings, lanyards and harnesses.

The following points should be considered in relation to the use of equipment based on webbing tape:

- Stitching may be in a contrasting shade or colour to that of the webbing to facilitate its inspection.
- Webbing equipment should preferably be supplied with pre-stitched identification labels to assist individual identification for inspection and recording purposes. Where this is not possible, the manufacturer should be contacted for advice before webbing articles are marked or labels attached.

3.4.2 Webbing Slings

Webbing slings are often preferred over rope when loads are passed over edges as the load is distributed over the whole width of the tape, which reduces the load on individual fibres. Protected webbing slings, therefore, are used extensively for wrapping around objects creating anchors to which a rope system may be secured. Webbing tape does not absorb shock loads as effectively as dynamic rope.

Webbing slings take the form of loops in various lengths made from flat or tubular webbing tape

pre-formed and pre-stitched into slings with a certificated safe working load.

The following points should be considered in relation to the use of equipment based on webbing tape:

- Webbing capable of creating a sling with a minimum rated static strength of 22 kilonewtons (kN) should be used.
- Stitching should be in a contrasting shade or colour to that of the webbing to facilitate its inspection. Stitching should only be carried out by a competent person, normally a commercial supplier.
- Webbing equipment should preferably be supplied with pre-stitched identification labels to assist individual identification for inspection and recording purposes. Where this is not possible, the manufacturer should be contacted for advice before webbing articles are marked or labels attached.
- A repair to webbing tape is normally not possible, the item being disposed of if damaged.

3.4.3 Lanyards

Lanyards are short lengths of dynamic rope, or textile webbing, usually terminating in a connector at either end. Their primary use is to secure a person to an anchor to prevent a fall, acting as a link between the anchor and the harness. To achieve this they must be able to withstand any shock loads that may be imposed on them. Webbing lanyards incorporate an energy absorber that slows the fall thus reducing the shock load on the anchor and should meet the requirements of BS EN355. Dynamic rope lanyards achieve the same outcome through the physical properties of the rope, which should be a minimum of 10.5 mm in diameter and meet the requirements of BS EN892. The length of the lanyard should be as short as practicable and the overall length including connectors normally limited to the length of the operator's reach.

Lanyards may also be used for other purposes such as work restraint, maintaining a link between a rescue operator and a stretcher or casualty. Specialised lanyards are available for use when climbing open structures such as vertical ladders, masts, tower cranes or scaffolding.

3.4.4 Safety and Work Harnesses

The primary functions of a harness are to support the wearer's body whilst suspended from a rope or to spread the load in the event of a fall. In view of the variation in sizes of potential users, harnesses must be capable of sufficient adjustment to provide and maintain an acceptable lever of comfort. Harnesses should comply with relevant standards appropriate to the intended use.

3.4.4.1 Work-positioning Harness

In situations where fire-fighters must work suspended from a rope or where the rope is supporting most of their bodyweight, a suitable harness must be considered. Harnesses designed for work positioning must support the wearer in a comfortable working position whilst allowing unhindered operation of other devices in the system. This is particularly important where the harness is to be used in conjunction with breathing apparatus in which case the provision of a suitable elevated attachment point is essential to maintain the operator in an upright position. The relevant standards are EN813 for sit harnesses and EN358 for work positioning.

Sit harnesses and full body harnesses suitable for work positioning also provide an alternative to the safety belt for work restraint e.g. travel restriction.

3.4.4.2 Fall Arrest Harness

In all operational situations where there is a risk of a fall that may result in injury, it is recommended that those at risk wear a suitable fall arrest harness complying with BS EN361. Fall arrest harnesses are usually fitted with chest or dorsal attachment points and either may be used dependent upon circumstances. In many cases, following a suitable risk assessment, fire and rescue services may find that a fall arrest harness is also suitable for work positioning use.

Whilst most sit harnesses can be converted to fall arrest standard by the addition of an appropriate chest harness, it should be noted that such a combination should be tested as a complete unit to BS EN361.

3.4.4.3 Casualty Harness

There are many types of harness available for casualty rescue. They range from simple slings or rescue strops to full body harnesses. When selecting a rescue harness, care should be taken to ensure that it is quick and simple to deploy, that it will provide an adequate level of support, reassurance for the casualty and that it is compatible with other equipment and Personal Protective Equipment (PPE) that may already be in use.

3.4.4.4 Safety Belts

A waist belt complying with the requirements of BS EN358 is sufficient for work restraint, e.g. preventing a fire-fighter from accessing a position where a fall might occur. These belts are inappropriate where personnel are suspended on a rope or where a fall might occur. Suitable belts based on webbing tape are broad or have padding for support and a locking buckle that cannot be accidentally released. A connector attaches the wearer to a suitable anchor, lanyard or the rope.

3.5 Metal-based Equipment

3.5.1 General

Increasing industrial and leisure use has led to many advances in the use of steel, high-grade alloy, plastic and carbon-fibre components in rope work systems. These components have many uses in the fire and rescue service, from the simplest system to the most complicated, including:

- Connectors, linking other components and ropes together.
- Rope Control Devices that act on the rope itself usually by means of friction.
- Pulleys, for reducing friction or applying mechanical advantage.
- Wire Strops, as part of anchor systems.
- Tripods, Quadpods and Frames, to alter the direction of rope travel.

Note: Do not drop metal-based items of equipment. The shock of equipment striking a solid surface with force can cause damage, undetectable by normal methods of examination, which may significantly weaken it.

Some alloy steel components can be affected by acidic or alkaline atmospheres, which may weaken the metal sufficiently that it becomes brittle and could fail if subject to a shock loading. This is termed 'hydrogen embrittlement'. Items suspected of being so affected, should be withdrawn from service for inspection by a competent person.

3.5.2 Connectors (karabiners, safety hooks, screw links)

These metal load-bearing components are used in nearly all rope systems. The purpose of a connector is to link together the various parts of the rope system. Each connector has a gate into which equipment can be inserted, the gate is then closed to prevent accidental disconnection. Connectors with a gate that cannot inadvertently open, e.g. screwgate or self-locking, are the only types that can provide the required level of security for fire and rescue service use. Connectors that are to be used with any fixed anchor such as a hangar, eyebolt or shackle should be of such a design and size that they are able to rotate freely in the anchor without hindrance and without loosening the anchor. Connectors used for static rigging and personal attachments should conform to BS EN 362 or a similar standard. A minimum strength of 25 kN (in the direction of maximum loading) is recommended for karabiners, safety hooks, and screw links.

3.5.2.1 Karabiners

May be constructed from steel or metal alloys, are usually oval or 'D' shaped and are designed to be loaded along the longitudinal axis only, i.e. along the spine. If the load is applied to the transverse axis or is offset from the spine, the weaker, 'gated' side of the connector may fail under a load less than specified for the component. Care should, therefore, be taken to ensure that karabiners do not become 'cross loaded' whilst in use and have a suitable factor of safety by using connectors of a

higher quoted strength than the minimum of 15 kN specified in BS EN 362.

3.5.2.2 Safety hooks

Provide for quick connections between two components and are used where a link has to be connected and disconnected regularly i.e. a lanyard connecting a harness to a structure. The gate on these hooks should be automatic of spring-loaded thus preventing accidental disconnection.

3.5.2.3 Screw links (also known as Maillon Rapides or Quick Links)

Are made from alloy or steel, usually delta, oval or 'D' shaped. The 'gate' is provided by a screw mechanism that makes them slower is use than karabiners. They have the advantage, however, of the closed gate being as strong as the other sides. Therefore, they offer more security when cross loaded as long as the gate is securely shut. In situations where a load may be applied in more than one direction or axis a suitable maillon or screw link should be used in preference to a karabiner.

3.5.3 Pulleys

These are devices with a grooved wheel (sheave) used to reduce friction. This reduction in friction is achieved by a combination of the rotational movement of the sheave and the increased radius around which the rope runs. The optimum size of the sheave is four times the diameter of the rope. Their construction is such that a connector can be attached, usually through side plates. In most modern designs the side plates swing to allow the pulley to be attached at any point along the rope (commonly known as 'swing cheek pulleys'). Pulleys come in a variety of designs and sizes including some that are large enough to allow knotted ropes to pass through them. The relevant standard is EN12278.

Pulleys containing more than one sheave are known as pulley blocks. The block being the shell or body in which the sheaves are housed.

3.5.4 Wire Strops

Wire strops can be made from lengths of wire rope with formed eyes at each end for the attachment of a connector. They are particularly useful when the chosen anchor is made of abrasive material or has sharp edges (e.g. brick piers or steelwork) that may cut or abrade rope or webbing tape slings.

3.5.5 General Metal Hardware

This may include ground anchors, rigging plates or any other piece of equipment designed to be used in conjunction with rope or anchor systems. Equipment should conform to relevant standards. If no standard is available then the fire and rescue service is responsible for ensuring that any equipment is used in accordance with manufacturer's instructions and that a competent person performs a risk assessment as to the suitability of the equipment.

3.5.6 Rope Control Devices

For the purposes of classification, rope control devices may be split into four types:

- Devices intended primarily for belaying.
- Devices intended primarily for lowering or descending.
- Devices intended primarily for hauling or ascending.
- Devices intended primarily for backing up the failure of another device or system.

Due to the versatility of many of the devices described below, some can be used for purposes other that their primary role. One device may, for example, be able to act as either an ascender or as a rope brake in a back up system, whilst another may be suitable as a belay/lowering device or as an abseil device.

When these types of equipment are put to any use other than their 'primary' use, users should ensure the manufacturer has guaranteed the device will operate in the manner they wish to use it.

3.5.6.1 Devices intended primarily for belaying

There is a broad range of devices available that are designed for use when controlling a rope by belaying. The vast majority of these devices are designed primarily for sports use and rely for their effective operation on friction being applied to the rope by direct positive manual action by the belayer. Whilst such devices provide a simple method of controlling a rope, they cannot in themselves be relied upon to 'fail safe'. It is, therefore, recommended that where belay devices are being used to control the lifting or lowering of persons or to provide safety backup, only those devices that are designed to auto-lock (i.e. fail safe) should be considered suitable for general use by Fire & Rescue Services.

3.5.6.2 Devices intended primarily for lowering or descending

These devices, commonly known as 'descenders', are used to attach an operator to the main working rope allowing the operator to control their own descent. They may also be attached to the anchor point and used remotely to lower an operator or load.

Descenders should:
- Give the user suitable control over the speed of descent.
- Be such that if the user loses control, they will stop or allow only a slow, controlled descent in the hands-off position.
- Be designed to 'fail safe' in operation.

Descenders should not:
- Cause significant abrasion or damage to the sheath when suddenly clamped onto the working line.
- Cause undue shock loads to the working rope when braking.
- Be capable of accidentally detaching from the working line.
- Be capable of being detached under any circumstances while carrying a person's weight.

When choosing a descender, brigades should bear in mind its suitability for use in the environmental conditions (e.g. wet, muddy, icy, abrasive, or corrosive) that are likely to prevail

Where long descents are likely, descenders should have good heat-dissipating properties to prevent burning of the operator's hands or heat damage to the working rope. They should also minimise twisting of the rope. Whenever any device is being used to support a load and a hands free situation is required, the device must be physically locked off to prevent uncontrolled adjustment.

Descenders should normally comply with BS EN 341.

3.5.6.3   Devices intended primarily for hauling or ascending

These devices, commonly known as 'ascenders' or 'rope grabs' may be used when the operator wishes to grip the rope for the purpose of hauling or ascending.

Ascenders generally fall into one of two groups, i.e. those that work by means of a toothed cam that grips onto the sheath or 'mantle' of the rope and those that utilise a toothless profiled cam that operates by compression of the rope. It should be noted that all cam devices have the potential to damage rope if shock loaded or operated with excessive loads. Ascenders should be of a type that cannot be accidentally detached from the rope and should be chosen so that the risk of damage to the rope is minimised when in use. When choosing a suitable ascender, Fire & Rescue Services should consider its suitability for use in the environmental conditions that are likely to prevail.

3.5.6.2   Devices intended primarily for backing up the failure of another device or system

These devices may be used when personnel working on a rope need a secondary device connected to an additional rope to provide a safety system should there be a failure in the primary system.

They operate such that they will move along the second rope as the operator ascends/descends the primary rope but will grab the rope should there be a sudden movement instigated by the individual falling due to the primary system failing.

To reduce the shock loading that occurs when these devices activate to arrest a fall, they should be monitored to ensure that any slack between the device and the individual is kept to a minimum

These devices should normally comply with E.N. 353-2.

It should be noted that devices intended for hauling/ascending and devices intended for backing up work in similar ways. It is important that any device used for these purposes should be assessed prior to use as to its suitability and used in line with its manufacturer's guidelines.

3.5.7   Tripods/Quadpods/Frames

These are portable frames that provide high attachment points to assist with access to a hazard zone for rescue purposes, or to allow loads to be lifted or lowered from ground level. There are many variations available, including tripods (3 legs), quadpods (4 legs), 'A' frames (2 legs) and specialist luffing frames. Tripods and quadpods generally have adjustable legs to allow them to be positioned on uneven ground. When selecting suitable devices, consideration should be given to the environment in which the equipment will be used. Systems such as tripods for example, are primarily designed to be used for a vertical lower or lift over an access point such as a sewer access or silo hatch. Others are designed specifically to provide a projection for access over an edge such as at a cliff. This is frequently referred to as an artificial high directional.

It should be borne in mind that this type of equipment can be subjected to high physical stresses in certain operational situations such as when lifting or lowering loads. Extreme care must, therefore, be taken when using these devices to ensure that they are effectively anchored to prevent movement or slippage. This is especially important when operating on unstable or uneven surfaces or on sloping ground.

3.5.8 Stretchers

There are two types of stretcher in common use:

● Rigid.

● Flexible.

3.4.8.1 Rigid stretchers

These are either moulded from plastic material or constructed from metal (normally aluminium alloy or stainless steel), though a combination of materials may be used. Due to their rigidity, this type of stretcher is not well suited for work in confined spaces and is normally deployed for rescues in open air. Rigid stretchers can either be one piece (e.g. a preformed basket stretcher) or sectional (requiring assembly prior to use).

3.5.8.2 Flexible stretchers

Usually comprise a plastic frame or sheet with a fabric cover and textile webbing attachments and have a limited degree of inherent rigidity. This type of stretcher is designed to wrap around the casualty and gains additional rigidity once the casualty has been secured within it. The inherent flexibility of these stretchers makes them ideal for use in confined spaces. Flexible stretchers are usually supplied in a custom made bag or valise and require minimal stowage space.

Most stretchers can be supplied with additional equipment for casualty packaging, including head support blocks, casualty harnesses and integral head protection.

Stretchers can be attached to a rope system by the use of slings and connectors, or specially designed strops. These can normally be used in a range of configurations allowing the stretcher to be hauled or lowered at any angle between vertical and horizontal.

When selecting a stretcher, consideration should be given to the environment in which it will be used and the uses to which it will be put. Particular care must be taken (when appropriate) to ensure compatibility with helicopters or for water rescues.

3.6 Ropes

3.6.1 General

There are many operational activities where the use of rope is necessary to achieve tasks or objectives. Rope may be used as part of a safe system of work in a variety of situations, for example to:

● Secure items such as branches or salvage sheets.
● Stabilise vehicles or ladders.
● Move loads, e.g. equipment, people or animals by hauling, lifting or lowering.
● Use safety ropes when working near unguarded edges.
● Work at height or in confined spaces.
● Carry out specialist rescues.

The general description given to all forms of fibre rope is cordage, which may be referred to as either a rope or a line depending on its particular application. FRS terminology refers to ropes cut to specific lengths for particular purposes as lines, although the term rope is more generally used for specialist rescue activities.

British Standard BS 3367:1999 refers to 'ropes and lines for fire service use other than for rope rescue purposes'. The Standard sets out the specification for rope that is used in the manufacture a range of fire and rescue service lines, which are to be made from polyester, and general purpose lines that may be made from polyester or polypropylene. The Standard does not apply to:

● Ropes used in conjunction with specialist rope rescue equipment.
● Guidelines and personal lines for use with breathing apparatus.

Ropes complying with BS 3367:1999, should have a ferrule or sleeve permanently marked with:

● The manufacturer's name, trademark or identification mark.
● The material, the nominal size of the rope and date of manufacture or batch number of the coil from which the rope was made.
● The number of the relevant British Standard.

3.6.1.1 Rope Construction

The properties and capabilities of rope are dependent upon both the material and the type of construction. Analysis of these factors will allow assessment of the most appropriate rope for each situation. In selecting the most suitable type of rope for a task it is important to consider the following:

- Physical characteristics, including tensile strength, weight, flexibility and texture.
- Ability of the rope to absorb the energy of shock loads.
- Ability of the rope to withstand repeated shock loadings.
- Degree of elongation under load.
- Degree of absorption of water and other liquids.
- Resistance to physical and chemical damage.

Natural Fibres

Fire and rescue service ropes were traditionally made from natural fibres such as Italian hemp, manila, sisal, coir and cotton. Whilst some of these ropes may still be in use they have generally been superseded by those made from synthetic materials.

Natural Fibre
Desirable Characteristics
● None
Undesirable Characteristics
● Low shock absorption
● Loss of strength when wet (up to 50%)
● High absorption of water
● Poor resistance to chemicals
● Loses strength over time
● Lower breaking strength than synthetic rope

Nylon

Ropes made from polyamide (nylon) are considered most suitable for the vast majority of fire and rescue service applications and should normally be considered for rope access, rescue or personal safety use.

Nylon
Desirable Characteristics
● Good shock absorption
● Fairly high melting point
● Good resistance to abrasion
● Resistant to alkalis and other chemicals
● Low surface friction
Undesirable Characteristics
● Can be seriously damaged by certain corrosives e.g. acids
● Loss of strength when wet (up to 15%)

Polyester

Ropes made from polyester (terylene) offer a suitable alternative to those made from nylon, however, as polyester is less able to absorb shock loadings it is generally not used in situations where substantial falls may occur. It may, however, be appropriate in specific circumstances for example, where chemical pollution is present.

Polyester
Desirable Characteristics
● High tensile strength even when wet
● Fairly high melting point
● Good resistance to abrasion
● Resistant to damage from acids and organic compounds
Undesirable Characteristics
● Can be seriously damaged by certain corrosives, e.g. alkalis
● Poor shock absorption (compared to nylon)

Polyolefin

Ropes manufactured from polyolefins such as high modulus polyethylene and high tenacity polypropylene are often used in water rescue because of their buoyancy. Polyolefins are not very strong and cannot absorb shock well, so most water rescue ropes combine these fibres with nylon to provide strength.

Aramid Fibre

This is generally known as 'Kevlar' and has great tensile strength, although it is not considered suitable for general rope construction.

Wire Rope

Certain working environments including marine, structural collapses and some confined space incidents may produce a higher potential for damage to textile rope. In these situations the use of wire rope may be preferred. In many respects the systems used with wire rope will be similar to those used for textile ropes, although control equipment is specific to wire rope. Wire ropes frequently require some form of mechanical system to control the movement of the rope. A wire rope system that may be subject to a shock load should include suitable energy absorbing equipment.

3.6.1.2 Types of Construction

There are three types of construction for ropes used in the fire service:

- Hawser Laid.
- Plaited.
- Kernmantel.

Hawser Laid Rope

Rope manufactured by twisting individual yarns into strands, a number of which are then twisted together in the opposite direction to form the finished rope. This has the effect of ensuring that the individual yarns do not become untwisted and that the load is evenly distributed throughout the rope.

The process of twisting the individual strands to make a hawser laid rope is known as 'laying up'. Ropes may be 'laid up' either right-hand (known as 'Z lay'), or left-hand (known as 'S lay') respectively. (See Figure 3.3.)

Figure 3.3 Diagram showing hawser laid rope in traditional 'S' and 'Z' lays.

Plaited Rope

This construction method involves plaiting the strands either in a single or double layer around a central core, which has the benefit of producing a smoother and more flexible construction. The two main types of construction are:

- 8-plait rope having a core of any construction encased in a sheath made from eight interlacing plaits, four in a clockwise direction and four in an anticlockwise direction.

- 16-plait rope having a parallel core encased in an 8-plait initial sheath, comprising eight interlacing plaits, four in a clockwise direction and four in an anticlockwise direction and comprising a secondary braided sheath made from 16 interlacing plaits, eight in a clockwise direction and eight in an anticlockwise direction. (See Figure 3.4.)

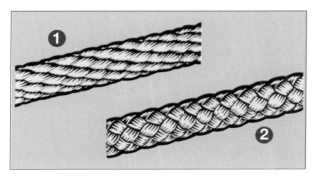

Figure 3.4 Diagram of plaited rope.

Kernmantel Rope

Kernmantel rope comprises a central core of continuous filaments known as the kern, which is the predominant load-bearing element. This is surrounded by a woven outer sheath known as the mantle, which shares a portion of the load, but has the primary role of protecting the core from abrasion and the ingress of dirt and grit. (See Figure 3.5.)

Kernmantel ropes may be supplied pre-treated to decrease the absorption of water and other chemicals. They can be supplied in a variety of colours and markings that may assist in rope identification and with tracking of the rope through rope control devices whilst in use. In order to suit a variety of applications, kernmantel ropes are manufactured as either low stretch or dynamic.

Low Stretch Ropes

Where ropes are being used for descent or lowering and a shock load is not anticipated, the working rope and the safety rope should be low-stretch and should meet the requirements of the European standard for low-stretch kernmantel ropes, BS EN 1891:1998.

Figure 3.5 Diagram of Kernmantel rope construction.

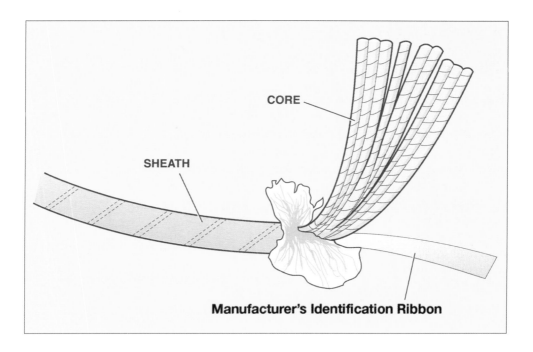

There are two categories of rope covered by this standard, i.e. types: A and B. Only ropes meeting the requirements of BS EN 1891: type A, should be used for rope access, work positioning and work restraint, including rescue or for any purpose involving the lifting or lowering of people.

Dynamic Ropes

These ropes are designed and manufactured to stretch when placed under load, dependent on the length of rope between the anchor point and the applied load this may be up to 40% of the original length.

Where ropes are used to arrest a potential fall i.e. lead climbing, and the possibility of a substantial shock loading exists, dynamic rope complying with BS EN 892:1997 should be used.

3.6.2   Categories of Rope

3.6.2.1   General Purpose Ropes

British Standard 3367:1999 specifies that general-purpose ropes for fire and rescue service use should be made from 16mm nominal diameter hawser laid polyester or polypropylene. Subject to a risk assessment that shows it is 'suitable for purpose', other rope may be appropriate for general-purpose usage. Examples of general-purpose ropes are:

- Long lines, ropes usually of 30m in length, used for securing or hauling equipment aloft and creating barriers around hazard zones.
- Short lines, ropes, 15m in length, used in applications where a long line would prove cumbersome such as securing suction hose to an appliance.

General purpose rope must not be used for personal safety or the lifting or lowering of persons. It is acknowledged, however, that circumstances of urgent operational need may arise where there is:

- An immediate threat to human life or safety. **and**
- The correct equipment is not readily available. **and**
- Inaction would result in death or serious injury.

In these circumstances, subject to a dynamic risk assessment, general-purpose ropes may be used until specific rescue equipment becomes available at the incident.

Smaller diameter rope, between 3mm and 8mm diameter, often in the form of a pocket line, may be used for attaching or securing equipment but must not be used in safety critical applications.

Cordage of kernmantel construction, between 3mm and 8mm diameter, is commonly known as accessory cord (Prusik line). Whilst this may be used as part of a specialist or rescue application, an appropriate risk assessment must be applied to ensure that it is fit for purpose.

Accessory cord tied into a loop (prusik loop) must have a manufacturer's certificate of conformity and safe working load if it is to be used in circumstances covered by LOLER.

3.6.2.1   Ropes for Rescue or Personal Fall Protection Systems

Textile ropes suitable for rescue or personal fall protection systems will generally be of kernmantel construction. A nominal diameter of 10.5 to 13 millimetres with a minimum tensile strength of 2500 Kg is recommended.

3.6.2.2   Floating Ropes for Use in Water Rescues

This type of rope is specifically designed for use in connection with water-based activities. Unlike natural fibre ropes that have a degree of buoyancy, the man made alternatives will float even after submersion in water for long periods of time. Sizes range from 5mm for lightweight throw lines to 16mm for general-purpose ropes.

Construction may be plaited or kernmantel design, with a polyester sheath to provide abrasion and heat resistance and a polypropylene core to maintain buoyancy. These ropes will not shrink when wet.

Figure 3.6 Photograph showing a variety of types of rope and cordage including kernmantel rope; British Standard 16mm hawser laid polyester GP line and an example of floating rope.

3.6.3 Associated Rope Working Equipment

The equipment that is connected to or that acts upon the rope is of equal importance to the rope itself in creating a safe system of work. Rope equipment can be classified by the material it is constructed from:

- Textile based equipment, e.g. webbing, harnesses and lanyards.
- Metal based equipment, e.g. karabiners, rope control devices and pulleys.
- Equipment constructed from metal, plastics and textiles, e.g. stretchers.

3.7 Equipment Identification

Equipment used for work at height must be uniquely identifiable for inspections, tests and tracking purposes. Requirements for identification of equipment should be specified when it is procured. Where a fire and rescue service wishes to add further identification to equipment the method and location of marking must be in accordance with instructions from the manufacturer or supplier.

- Marking pens may chemically damage textile items and must not be used unless approved by the supplier of the equipment.

- Stamping or etching may physically damage or weaken metal items if carried out on load bearing components.

FRS should have a system in place, which will ensure that equipment not designed for lifting or lowering persons cannot be used for such a purpose. Whilst ropes and rope equipment that are suitable for the lifting and lowering of persons can be used for other purposes, fire and rescue services may wish to restrict these applications in order to minimise damage caused by excessive or shock loads, or the risk of contamination by oil or chemicals.

3.8   Stowage of Ropes and Associated Equipment

Correct stowage of rope and associated equipment is the second stage in an effective maintenance regime. All rope equipment should be kept clean, dry and free from contamination in a cool place out of direct sunlight. Care should be taken to ensure that ropes and equipment that will be used for rescue or for any purpose involving the lifting or lowering of persons, are stowed well clear of oil, grease or chemicals and are not allowed to come into direct contact with hot surfaces.

Equipment may be best stowed grouped and bagged ready for use to ensure that no essential item is left behind. Bags may be colour coded for ease of identification and may be marked with a description of the contents.

Stowing equipment in this way serves several purposes:

- The equipment is ready for immediate use.
- The equipment is protected from deterioration caused by exposure to ultra-violet light.
- The equipment is protected from mechanical damage.
- The equipment is protected from chemical damage.
- The equipment is easily identified.

The equipment may be readily transported to the scene of operations and is immediately available for use.

3.9   Equipment Inspections, Examinations and Tests

The inspection of working at height equipment is detailed in Regulation 12 and specifies general inspection requirements. All equipment for work at height must be subject to a structured inspection or test regime.

All equipment should be thoroughly examined after use and where necessary washed and dried before re-stowage. Cleaning and stowage should be in accordance with the manufacturer's instructions.

The appropriate method of inspecting equipment for work at height is by visual and tactile examination. Load testing of equipment must only be undertaken in line with specific instructions provided by the supplier.

3.9.1   Pre-use and after-use checks

All equipment that may be used for work at height must be checked to ensure that its condition is appropriate for its intended use:

- After each occasion of use, e.g. operational incident or training session.
- Before every training session where the potential failure of any component could have life safety implications.
- At suitable intervals between detailed inspections.
- Generally personnel who have received training in the use of equipment can be considered competent to undertake inspections and pre-use checks.

3.9.2   Detailed Inspection

All equipment must be thoroughly examined by a competent person:

- Before being brought into use for the first time.
- In accordance with any pre-determined examination scheme.
- If it has been involved in an accident, near miss or dangerous occurrence.

When prescribing a thorough examination as part of an inspection routine, the competent person must:

- Take account of manufacturer's and supplier's guidance.
- Consider the frequency and environment of use of the equipment.

Competent persons should have practical and theoretical knowledge and experience of the equipment that is to be examined. This will enable them to detect defects or weaknesses and assess their likely effect on the continued safe use of the equipment. Competent persons must also have sufficient independence of authority to allow decisions to be made on the continued suitability of equipment. This does not mean the competent persons must come from independent organisations, rather that "in house" examiners are given genuine authority and independence to ensure that examinations are completed correctly and that any subsequent recommendations are implemented.

Interim inspections may be needed between detailed inspections when risk assessments have identified that there could be a significant deterioration, affecting the safety of the equipment before the next detailed inspection is due. The need for and frequency of interim inspections will depend on the level and environment of use, including exposure to potential contaminants.

3.9.3 Maintenance

It is essential that all equipment used for work at height operations is maintained in efficient working order and good repair. Maintenance regimes should be:

- Planned preventative – where adjustments are made and parts replaced at pre-set intervals.
- Condition based – where the condition of safety critical parts are regularly monitored and repaired or replaced as required.
- Carried out or supervised by a competent person.

Guidance from manufacturers and suppliers must be incorporated into prescribed maintenance and inspection regimes.

3.9.4 Record Keeping

The following information should be kept and made available for inspection for as long as the equipment is available for use:

- Certificate of conformity.
- All reports of detailed inspections.
- All reports of defects.
- Records of routine inspections.

Each report of a detailed inspection should include the following information (WaHR Regulation 12):

- The name and address of the employer for whom the detailed inspection was made.
- The address of the premises where the detailed inspection was made.
- Information sufficient to identify the equipment including serial numbers.
- In accordance with timescales specified by an examination scheme, or after the occurrence of exceptional circumstances.
- That the lifting equipment would be safe to operate or otherwise.
- Identification of any part found to have a defect that is or could become a danger to persons and a description of the defect.
- Particulars of any repair, renewal or alteration required to remedy a defect found to be a danger to persons.
- In the case of a defect which is not yet but could become a danger to persons, the time by which it could become such a danger and particulars of any repair, renewal or alteration required to remedy the defect.
- The date of the detailed inspection.
- The name of the person signing or authenticating the report.
- The date of the report.

Records should be kept at the premises of use but where this proves impractical they may be held at a central location. They must still, however, remain available for inspection. There is no requirement to keep a record of pre-use checks.

3.9.5 Disposal of Equipment

Any item of equipment used for work at height which reaches the end of the manufacturer's recommended life expectancy or fails an inspection and cannot be repaired, should be removed from service and be destroyed to prevent re-use. In order to assist brigades discharging their general duty of care the principles of safe disposal should be considered when any item of equipment is withdrawn from service.

Chapter 4 – Training

4.1 General Requirements

In order for individuals to work safely at height it is important that a systematic process is in place to ensure that personnel are properly trained and they demonstrate possession of the necessary knowledge, skills and understanding.

Fire and rescue services should implement specific training programmes for personnel to achieve and maintain the required level of competence for work at height. Each fire and rescue service will need to determine the boundary between core skills applicable to all personnel who work at height and the more technical skill required of staff who undertake specialist duties. Appropriate levels of training in specialist activities cannot easily be achieved for all personnel.

Specific good practice guidance on training for work at Height is provided by:

- The Health and Safety Executive, through their Work at Height Syllabus prepared by the Advisory Committee on Work at Height Training (www.acwaht.org.uk).
- BS 8454:2006: Code of practice for the delivery of training and education for work at height and rescue.

4.1.1 Training Structure

Training programmes should include:

- Initial training, to acquire the required knowledge skills and understanding, along with assessment of initial development.
- Continuation training, to provide ongoing assessment of individual and team levels of knowledge skills and understanding.

- Continuing professional development (CPD), to provide a point in time review of knowledge, skills and understanding.

The training needs of individuals, their level of experience, and the circumstances of local work environments will dictate the quantity and frequency of training activities. All specialist technical training activities should be planned and conducted by a competent technical supervisor or instructor.

Model training aims and objectives for work at height are outlined under the following headings:

- Knowledge skills and understanding required by all firefighters.
- Training for specialist rope operator support duties.
- Training for specialist rope operator duties.
- Rope work supervisor training.
- Rope work instructor training.
- Continuation and CPD training.
- Ongoing assessment.

4.1.2 Instructors

Fire and rescue services that undertake technical specialist rope work activities should appoint a senior rope work instructor who will be responsible for:

- Validating the technical aspects of rope. working and the suitability of equipment.
- Assessing the knowledge, skills and understanding of other instructors.
- Supervising the conduct and assessment of specialist rope operator courses.

Fire and rescue services must ensure that rope work instructors are competent and have appropriate experience. When this is not available within the fire and rescue service, consideration should be given to:

- The use of competent instructors from other fire and rescue services.
- Provision of training by external training providers.

4.2 Training Requirements for all Firefighters

Training for safe work at height should be provided at trainee stage. Where FRSs operate specialised rope work equipment, familiarisation should also be provided. It may also be appropriate for elements of more specialised training to be provided where there is a realistic probability that such skills will be generally required. In these circumstances fire and rescue services should add the relevant parts of specialist training described in later paragraphs.

Training Aims
Knowledge Skills and Understanding Required by all Firefighters

Prior Learning	Practical Skills
Aim 1	Recognise circumstances where work at height may lead to the risk of a fall and implement appropriate safety systems.
Aim 2	Use ropes to secure equipment and other items.
Aim 3	Understand the practical application of general lifting and lowering techniques and apply them in practice.
Aim 4	Inspect and maintain ropes and associated equipment in general use.

Aim 1
Recognise circumstances where work at height may lead to the risk of a fall and implement appropriate safety systems.

Knowledge and Understanding	Practical Skills
Requirements of the Work at Height Regulations 2005. Specific guidance can be found in the HSE Work at Height Syllabus prepared by the Advisory Committee on Work at Height Training (www.acwaht.org.uk).	Select and use work practices that avoid work at height. Select and use equipment to prevent the risk of a fall. Select and use work equipment to minimise the consequences of a fall.
Circumstances where actions should be taken to protect personnel from the risk of a fall. Use and limitations of different fall prevention and fall protection equipment and systems. Limitations of use for safety belts and harnesses.	Select and use appropriate collective or personal protection systems.
Suitable anchor points and their limitations.	Select and use suitable anchor points.
Capabilities and limitations of ropes, slings, connectors and associated equipment used for 'work restraint' and 'fall arrest' systems.	Use ropes, slings, connectors and associated equipment for 'work restraint' and 'fall arrest' systems.
Principles of safe practices for working near unguarded edges.	Apply safe practices for working near unguarded edges.

Aim 2
Use ropes to secure equipment and other items.

Knowledge and Understanding	Practical Skills
Application, use and limitations of ropes, knots and lashings.	Use ropes knots and lashings in a range of different contexts.
Capabilities and limitations of ropes in general use within the fire and rescue service.	

Aim 3
Understand the practical application of general lifting and lowering techniques and apply them in practice.

Knowledge and Understanding	Practical Skills
Meaning of Safe Working Load, Working Load Limit, Factor of Safety and associated terminology.	
Limitations imposed by manual handling requirements.	Apply systems using mechanical advantage to rope work activities.
Mechanical advantage.	
Use and limitations of attachments and ancillary equipment used for lifting purposes.	Use attachments and ancillary equipment for lifting purposes.

Aim 4
Inspect and maintain ropes and associated equipment in general use.

Knowledge and Understanding	Practical Skills
Inspection and maintenance requirements for ropes, harnesses and other webbing equipment.	Demonstrate the inspection and maintenance of ropes, harnesses and other webbing equipment.
Inspection and maintenance requirements for connectors, other hardware and ancillary equipment.	Demonstrate the inspection and maintenance of connectors, other hardware and ancillary equipment.
Stowage and transport of ropes, harnesses, other hardware and ancillary equipment.	Demonstrate the correct stowage and transport of ropes, harnesses, other hardware and ancillary equipment.

4.3 Specialist Rope Operator Support Duties

Personnel expected to work in this role should receive training specific to the use of specialised equipment. Such training need not be to the same extent as training required by operators, but should include such things as preparation prior to use, operational use, operational safety points and incident command principles.

Training Aims Specialist Rope Operator Support Duties	
Prior learning	**Possession of the knowledge, skills and understanding of rope working required by all firefighters.**
Aim 1	Identify, establish and manage the hazard zone above, adjacent to and below any working area.
Aim 2	Meet the equipment and support requirements of specialist rope work teams.
Aim 3	Undertake safety checks.
Aim 4	Set up and manage rope anchorage and belay points.
Aim 5	Inspect and maintain ropes and associated equipment.

Aim 1:
Identify, establish and manage the hazard zone above, adjacent to and below any working area

Knowledge and Understanding	Practical Skills
Principles and guidelines for setting up and managing a hazard zone.	Set up a hazard zone and demonstrate its management.
Methods of safe working within the hazard zone.	Demonstrate the methods of safe working within the hazard zone.

AIM 2:
Meet the equipment and support requirements of specialist rope work teams

Knowledge and Understanding	Practical Skills
Name and describe items of specialised rope working equipment.	Select items of specialised rope working equipment by name and description
Principles and guidelines for equipment management at an incident	Set up an equipment dump and demonstrate its management.
Principles of rope hauling and lowering systems.	Set up, monitor and operate rope hauling and lowering systems.
Principles of safety back-up systems.	Set up and monitor safety back-up systems.

AIM 3:
Undertake safety checks

Knowledge and Understanding	Practical Skills
Safety checks undertaken before a specialist rope work team operator descends a rope or ascends a structure.	Demonstrate the safety checks undertaken before a specialist rope work team operator descends a rope or ascends a structure.
Safety checks undertaken throughout the time that personnel are suspended from rope.	Demonstrate the safety checks undertaken throughout the time that personnel are suspended from rope.

AIM 4:
Set up and manage rope belay points and anchor systems

Knowledge and Understanding	Practical Skills
Various types of anchor system available for use and their limitations.	Set up and monitor a secure rope belay for each type of anchor.
Describe the issues to be taken into account when monitoring rope belays and anchors.	

AIM 5:
Inspect and maintain ropes and associated equipment in specialist use

Knowledge and Understanding	Practical Skills
Inspection and maintenance requirements for harnesses and other webbing equipment.	Inspect ropes, harnesses, other webbing equipment, connectors and ancillary equipment and demonstrate maintenance regimes.
Inspection and maintenance requirements for connectors and ancillary equipment.	
Stowage and transport of specialist ropes, harnesses and all associated equipment.	

4.4 Specialist Rope Operator Duties

Specialist rope work which involves activities in high and exposed situations, places particular demands on the individual, such that some people are not able to cope with the psychological or physiological demands involved. Members of specialist rope work teams must have the attitude and aptitude for such work. Selection and training processes should take account of:

- Medical, physical and psychological fitness to work in high and exposed locations. (Fire and rescue services may wish to use their occupational health screening facilities to identify these characteristics.)
- The need for specialist operators to work in difficult environments out of sight of their supervisors.
- The need for new trainees to be closely monitored.

- The need for individuals who experience signs of psychological or physiological difficulties to be identified and to be given the opportunity to address these problems or to withdraw or be withdrawn from specialist activities

After completing a course of initial training, specialist rope operators should undertake a further period of consolidation training which should:

- Be under the direct observation of a specialist rope work supervisor or instructor.
- Cover all specialist rope work activities.
- Conclude with a formal assessment of knowledge, skills and understanding, applied to range of simulated rescue scenarios.

Specialist operators should not be considered for specialist rope work duties in an operational context until the consolidation training and a formal practical assessment has been successfully completed.

Training Aims Specialist Rope Operator Duties	
Prior learning	Possession of the knowledge, skills and understanding required for specialist rope operator support duties.
Aim 1	Understand the hazards and risks associated with specialist rope activities and apply appropriate control measures in practical situations.
Aim 2	Access a scene of operations and return to the starting point using standard rope techniques.
Aim 3	Rescue a casualty.
Aim 4	Provide a safe work environment for other personnel, e.g. paramedics who may need to access the work area.

AIM 1:
Understand the hazards and risks associated with specialist rope activities and apply appropriate control measures in practical situations

Knowledge and Understanding	Practical Skills
General safety procedures.	Application of general safety procedures.
Principles of site management and incident command at specialist rope work incidents.	Apply the principles of site management and incident command at specialist rope work incidents.
Identify situations requiring the use of restraint, work positioning or fall arrest equipment.	Select the correct equipment and PPE for use in a range of specialist rope activities.
Identify appropriate PPE for a range of specialist rope activities.	
Fall factors and the dangers of excessive shock loads.	

AIM 2:
Access a scene of operations and return to the starting point using standard techniques

Knowledge and Understanding	Practical Skills
Equipment appropriate for use in a range of specialist activities.	Select and don the correct equipment for the task.
Safety checks undertaken before descent or ascent.	Undertake all safety checks necessary before descent or ascent.
Standard techniques for descending and ascending a rope and the application of a safety back-up system in a range of locations to meet local risks.	Use standard techniques to descend and ascend a rope and apply a safety back-up system in a range of locations to meet local risks.
Standard practices for ascending and descending a structure using fall-arrest techniques.	Ascend and descend a structure using fall-arrest techniques.
Improvised systems of work and the relevant safe working limits of equipment.	Use improvised systems of work within the safe working limits of equipment.
Additional rope techniques (e.g. cableways, hauling systems etc) that are appropriate to meet the full range of local risks and the anticipated requirements of incidents.	Use additional rope techniques (e.g. cableways, hauling systems etc) as appropriate to the range of local risks and anticipated requirements of incidents.

AIM 3:
Rescue a casualty

Knowledge and Understanding	Practical Skills
Standard techniques for rescue using a rescue harness or stretcher in a range the circumstances appropriate to local risks.	Rescue of a casualty from a range of different locations/ environments using a rescue harness or stretcher.
First aid and casualty handling to the standard required by Health and Safety First Aid at Work Regulations or any such equivalent first aid or casualty handling qualification in line with fire and rescue service policy.	Apply effective casualty care.
The range of injuries likely to be sustained by casualties and the implication for rescue techniques.	

AIM 4:
Provide a safe work environment for other personnel e.g. paramedics who may need to access the work area

Knowledge and Understanding	Practical Skills
Safety factors required to provide a safe work environment	Brief relevant people on all safety factors and confirm understanding.
PPE and systems of work to lower and recover other personnel to and from a work site.	Select appropriate PPE, lower other personnel to and from a work site and recover them to a safe place.

4.5 Rope Work Supervisor

The role of rope work supervisors is to:

- Supervise continuation training.
- Undertake assessment of the knowledge, skills and understanding of specialist rope operators on an ongoing basis.
- Act as team leaders at incidents.

Rope work supervisors should be drawn from personnel who have demonstrated competence as a specialist rope operator and in general instructional skills.

Supervisor status should be reviewed periodically. It is recommended that this process take place at least every three years and should include CPD.

Training Aims Rope Work Supervisor	
Prior learning	Possession of the knowledge, skills and understanding required to undertake specialist rope operator duties. Experience in undertaking the role of a specialist rope operator. Possession of general instructor skills.
Aim 1	Plan and conduct a continuation training session for personnel.
Aim 2	Give instruction on equipment and technical aspects of rope working.
Aim 3	Plan and supervise the activities of teams undertaking rope work activities.

AIM 1:
Plan and conduct a continuation training session for personnel

Knowledge and Understanding	Practical Skills
Identification of training needs, preparation of training sessions, assessment of performance and provision of feedback on specialist rope work activities.	Deliver a practical and a theoretical training session and demonstrate the assessment of performance.
	Identify training needs and prepare a lesson plan for a practical and a theoretical training session.
	Provide effective feedback on performance and identify any further training needs.

AIM 2:
Give instruction on equipment and technical aspects of rope working

Knowledge and Understanding	Practical Skills
Use of equipment, limitations as to use, safety factors, care and maintenance and safe systems of work	Prepare and deliver continuation training on equipment.
	Prepare and deliver continuation training on systems of work.
Fall factors and shock loads.	Describe the meaning of fall factors and explain their importance in relation to shock loads.

AIM 3:	
Plan and supervise the activities of teams undertaking rope work	
Knowledge and Understanding	**Practical Skills**
Application of specialist rope activities in operational situations.	Plan work and supervise work teams in operational situations.
Equipment maintenance, inspection and testing regimes.	Supervise equipment maintenance, inspection and testing regimes.

4.6   Rope Work Instructor

Individuals nominated for training as instructors for rope work, should be experienced rope work supervisors.

Rope work instructors will undertake the following roles:

- Initial training of specialist rope operators, supervisors and other instructors.
- Continuation training for supervisors and other instructors.
- Formal assessments of knowledge, skills and understanding for all operators, supervisors and instructors.

- Advise management on systems of work and equipment.

Fire and rescue services should appoint a competent person to co-ordinate and manage instructor training.

Rope work instructor status should be reviewed periodically. It is recommended that this process takes place annually and should include CPD.

Training aims and objectives should include:

Training Aims	
Rope Work Instructor	
Prior learning	Possession of the knowledge, skills and understanding required to undertake the role of a rope work supervisor. Experience in undertaking the role of a specialist rope work supervisor.
Aim 1	Provide training courses for all specialist rope operators, rope work supervisors and instructors.
Aim 2	Monitor the performance of rope work activities and give advice on procedures and equipment.

AIM 1:	
Provide training courses for all rope work operators, supervisors and instructors	
Knowledge and Understanding	**Practical Skills**
Identification of training needs, preparation of training sessions, assessment of performance and provision of feedback on specialist rope work activities.	Prepare and deliver specialist rope operator, supervisor and instructor initial training courses.
	Prepare training programmes and deliver supervisor and instructor continuation training courses
	Conduct performance assessments of specialist rope operators, supervisors and instructors, Give feedback and identify further training needs.

AIM 2:	
Monitor the performance of rope work activities and give advice on specialist procedures and equipment	
Knowledge and Understanding	**Practical Skills**
Maintenance and knowledge of developments in equipment, good practice and safe systems of work.	Review procedures, equipment and working practices on a regular basis. Provide guidance and advice on revisions.

4.7   Technical Rope Work Officer

The officer nominated to take overall management responsibility for technical rope work should ensure that an appropriate level of corporate knowledge is maintained and new developments are properly considered. Suitable activities will include:

- Attendance at seminars and conferences.
- Participation in User Groups.
- Attendance on appropriate courses provided by other brigades or recognised external trainers.
- Reviewing technical journals and manufacturers' information.
- Liaison with other agencies involved in rope working activities.

4.8   Continuation Training and CPD

4.8.1   General Requirements

Ongoing assessment of knowledge, skills and understanding is essential to ensure systems for safe work at height continue to be applied correctly. This should be undertaken in a structured and systematic way to ensure all aspects are addressed on a regular basis and that all relevant personnel are included. A specific programme should be in place for personnel who use ropes, harnesses and associated equipment in a more specialised technical way.

The more specialist aspects of rope working are by nature complex and critical in their application. It is essential, therefore, that the knowledge, skills and understanding of specialist rope operators is regularly assessed through a structured programme of activities.

Good practice developed in FRSs that have operated specialist rope rescue teams over a number of years indicates that CPD and continuation training will:

- Be structured and progressive to address the knowledge, skills and understanding required by specialist rope operators on a continuing basis.
- Include ongoing assessment of performance in practical skills, procedural knowledge and equipment management.

- Provide a minimum of six opportunities for each specialist rope operator to handle equipment and apply systems of work in a simulated rescue situation evenly distributed over each each twelve-month period.
- Provide more frequent opportunities for personnel with limited experience of specialist rope work to handle equipment and apply systems of work to simulated rescue situations.
- Provide an assessment of knowledge, skills and understanding for specialist rope operators who have been away from specialist duties in excess of twelve weeks or other period as determined by individual service policy. The assessment will either confirm competence to undertake operational duties or indicate the need for refresher training.
- Provide opportunities to develop new relevant knowledge, skills and understanding

4.9 Use of Live Casualties

When training for work at height, the part of the casualty or victim is generally best served by use of a training manikin. Manual handling considerations must be taken into account, particularly during the placement of a manikin for rescue. There are circumstances where risk to personnel in placing the manikin in a realistic rescue situation is such that the activity should preferably be avoided. Risk assessment of training sites will identify such locations.

There are times when the experience of working with or receiving continuous feedback from a live casualty is a key part of learning (e.g. for casualty handling) and the required learning outcomes cannot be met if a training manikin is used. A live casualty should be an individual competent to work at height.

When competent specialist personnel undertake the role of the casualty, valuable feedback on performance can be provided with safety observations and direct instructions being given as needed.

The guiding principles for the use of live casualties should ensure that:

- The use of live casualties is avoided unless essential to the outcomes required.
- Any exposure to risk is justified and effectively managed to achieve clear and established learning outcomes.
- The risk is not disproportionate to the benefits.
- The risk to the 'casualty' should not be greater than that to the rescuer.
- Live casualties are used when casualty care is the prime objective of the training session.
- Live casualties are provided with appropriate PPE, including a separate safety system as appropriate.

These same principles could be applied when assessing of the need for personnel to be trained to undertake a 'carry down' using fire service ladders. If it is determined that such an activity is foreseeable and training therefore needs to be provided, the technique of mounting a ladder carrying a live casualty could be practiced at low level on a purpose designed facility with appropriate fall protection in place.

If the purpose of the exercise is to practice descending a ladder carrying a load over a distance, then a simulated load could be used to represent the casualty and the individual undergoing the training could be protected with a fall arrest system as necessary.

Bibliography

Legislation

Attention is drawn to the following acts and regulations, and HSE approved codes of practice (ACoP) and guidance.

Health and Safety at Work etc. Act 1974.

Construction (Design and Management) Regulations 1994 (CDM Regulations) SI 199413 140 as amended and ACoP *Managing construction for health and safety* (HSE L54).

Work at Height Regulations 2005 (WAH Regulations) SI 2005/735.

Construction (Health, Safety and Welfare) Regulations 1996 (CHSW Regulations) SI 1996/1592 (as amended by the Work at Height Regulations 2005 SI 2005/735).

Construction (Head Protection) Regulations 1989 SI 1989/2209.

Electricity at Work Regulations 1989.

Health and Safety (First Aid) Regulations 1981.

Lifting Operations and Lifting Equipment Regulations 1998 (LOLER) SI 1998/2307 and ACoP and Guidance *Safe use of lifting equipment* 1998 (HSE L113).

Management of Health and Safety at Work Regulations 1999 (MHSW Regulations) SI 1999 13242 and ACoP *Management of health and safety at work* (HSE L21).

Personal Protective Equipment Regulations 2002 SI 200211 144.

Personal Protective Equipment at Work Regulations 1992 (PPE) SI 1992/2966 and amendments, and guidance document *Personal protective equipment at work* 1992 (HSE L25).

Provision and Use of Work Equipment Regulations 1998 (PUWER) SI 1998/2306 and ACoP Safe use of work equipment (HSE L22).

Workplace (Health, Safety and Welfare) Regulations 1992 SI 1992/3004 as amended and ACoP *Workplace health, safety and welfare* (HSE L24).

The Confined Spaces Regulations 1997, SI No. 1713 1997; ACoP and Guidance, *Safe work in confined spaces* (HSE) L101

HSE Guidance

HSG 150 Further information on guardrails (and working platforms).

HSE Information Sheet MISC614, Preventing Falls From Boom-type Mobile Elevating Work Platforms

HSE INDG 367 Inspecting Fall Arrest Equipment Made from Webbing or Rope.

HSE Information Sheet Construction Information Sheet No: 49 (Revision) General Access Scaffolds and Ladders

HSE Information Sheet Construction Information Sheet No: 10 (Revision 4) Tower Scaffolds.

Fire and Rescue Service specific

Fire & Rescue Manual Volume 4, Fire Service Training, Foundation Training & Development, 2004

HM Fire Service Inspectorate, 1998: Fire Service Guide 'Dynamic Management of Risk at Operational Incidents'
[HM Stationery Office 1998 ISBN 0 11 341221 5]

HM Fire Service Inspectorate, 1998: A Guide for Managers, Health and Safety, Fire Service guide Volume 2.
[The Stationery Office ISBN 0 11 3412193]

HM Fire Service Inspectorate, 1998: A Guide to Operational Risk Assessment, Fire Service Guide Volume 3
[HM Stationery Office 1998 ISBN 0 11 341220 7]

HM Fire Service Inspectorate, 2001: A Guide for Managers, Health and Safety, Fire Service Guide Volume 2, Module 18, Health and Safety Audit
[The Stationery Office ISBN 0 11 341248 7]

DCOL 05/2004 Item A: Guidance relating to personnel on decks of aerial appliances

DCOL 03/2004 Item E: Aerial Appliances – Provision of anchor devices.

British Standards Institution

Lifting Equipment

EN 696, *Fibre ropes for general service – Polyamide*
EN 697, *Fibre ropes for general service – Polyester*
EN 698, *Fibre ropes for general service – Manila and sisal*
EN 699, *Fibre ropes for general service – Polypropylene*
EN 1050:1996, *Safety of machinery – Principles of risk assessment*
EN 1261, *Fibre ropes for general service – Hemp*
EN 1677-1, *Components for slings – Safety – Part 1: Forged steel components, Grade 8*
EN 1677-2, *Components for slings – Safety – Part 2: Forged steel lifting hooks with latch, Grade 8*
EN 1677-3, *Components for slings – Safety – Part 3: Forged steel self-locking hooks, Grade 8*
EN 1677-4, *Components for slings – Safety – Part 4: Links, Grade 8*
EN 1677-5, *Components for slings – Safety – Part 5: Forged steel lifting hooks with latch, Grade 4*

EN 1677-6, *Components for slings – Safety – Part 6: Links, Grade 4*
EN 13411-1, *Terminations for steel wire ropes – Safety – Part 1: Thimbles for steel wire rope slings*
EN ISO 1968:2004, *Fibre ropes and cordage – Terms and definitions (ISO 1968:2004)*
EN ISO 7500-1:1999, *Metallic materials – Verification of static uniaxial testing machines – Part 1: Tension/compression testing machines (ISO 7500-1:1999)*
EN ISO 12100-2, *Safety of machinery – Basic concepts, general principles for design – Part 2: Technical principles (ISO 12100-2:2003)*

Fall Protection

BS EN 354, *Personal protective equipment against falls from a height – Lanyards.*
BS EN 355, *Personal protective equipment against falls from a height – Energy absorbers.*
BS EN 358:2000, *Personal protective equipment for work positioning and prevention of falls from a height – Belts for work positioning and restraint and work positioning lanyards.*
BS EN 360, *Personal protective equipment against falls from a height – Retractable type fall arresters.*
BS EN 361, *Personal protective equipment against falls from a height – Full body harnesses.*
BS EN 362, *Personal protective equipment against falls from a height – Connectors.*
BS EN 363, *Personal protective equipment against falls from a height – Fall arrest systems.*
BS EN 795:1997, *Protection against falls from a height – Anchor devices – Requirements and testing.*
BS EN 813, *Personal protective equipment for the prevention of falls from a height – Sit harnesses.*
BS EN 892:1996, *Mountaineering equipment – Dynamic mountaineering ropes – Safety requirements and test methods.*
BS EN 1497, *Personal fall protection equipment – Rescue harnesses.*
BS EN 1891:1998, *Personal protective equipment for the prevention of falls from a height – Low stretch kernmantel ropes.*
BS 8437:2005 – *Code of practice for selection, use and maintenance of personal fall protection systems and equipment for use in the workplace.*

IS0 1140: 1990, *Ropes – Polyamide – Specification.*
IS0 1141:1990, *Ropes – Polyester – Specification.*

Glossary

This Glossary refers to terminology that is likely to be encountered in relation to rope working and goes beyond the detail included in the main text of this document.

active rope/live rope
Rope tied to the harness of a moving rescuer or load and controlled by a belayer.

aid climbing
Progression by clipping into successive anchor points using short lanyards, etriers, and/or ropes, to gain access to higher or more difficult places.

anchor; anchor point
A safe point or object to which an individual or system may be securely attached.

anchor rope
Flexible rope connected at least at one end to a reliable anchor to provide a means of support, restraint or other safeguard for a person wearing a body support. An anchor rope may be a working rope or a safety rope.

ascender
A mechanical rope control device which, when attached to a rope of appropriate type and diameter, will slip freely in one direction but lock under load in the opposite direction.

back-up device
A rope control device for a safety rope of appropriate type and diameter, which accompanies the user during changes of position or allows adjustment of the length of the safety rope, and which locks automatically to the safety rope, or only allows gradual movement along it, when a sudden load occurs.

back-up rope; safety rope; secondary rope
Rope provided as a safeguard. This rope is used to protect against falls if the rope operator slips or if the primary support (e.g. the working rope), anchor or positioning mechanism fails.

belay
Place where ropes or people may be anchored or secured. The practice of providing safety backup by use of a rope and rope control device attached to an anchor.

belaying or life lining
Method of providing a safety rope to a person operating in a hazard area where a fall or slip is likely. The rope is controlled by a rope control device, operated by the belayer.

'below'	A warning that is shouted when any object is thrown, dropped or dislodged from a height and is applicable to all persons in the hazard area.
bight	The middle part of a length of rope. The term also applies to a loop of rope, and to 'make a bight' is to form a loop.
body support	A belt or harness used to attach a person to a rope or anchor point.
breaking load; failure load	The load which, when applied to an item of equipment when it is new will cause complete failure (previously called breaking strain).
cable way	Tensioned rope suspended between two points, along which rescuers and casualties may traverse.
clearance	Required distance below a person or load to prevent them/it striking the ground in the event of a fall, taking account of any energy absorber plus any stretch or give in the system.
connector	Openable device used to connect components of a rope working system.
cow's tail	Short strop, lanyard or sling connected to the main attachment point of a harness.
danger area	Defined in the Work at Height Regulations. Referred to in this document as a 'Hazard Zone'
descender	Manually operated, friction inducing, rope control device, which when attached to a rope of appropriate type and diameter, allows the user to achieve a controlled descent and (dependent on specific model) a stop at any point on a rope.
dogging the tails; rope dog	Consists of two 1 metre tails of rope at one end and a sewn eye at the other. When laced onto a working rope, it provides a method of attaching a hauling system while applying minimum damage to the rope. It works on a similar principle to a spliced rope. **Note:** Dogging the tails does not comply with LOLER unless given a SWL by supplier
dynamic rope	Rope specifically designed to absorb energy in a fall by extending in length, thereby minimising the impact force.
edge rollers	Pulley-type devices used at the edge of vertical or angled drops to reduce friction and also avoid rope abrasion.
edge protection	Within the context of the WAH Regulations 'edge protection' is a term used to describe physical barriers such as parapets, sills, guard rails etc.

energy absorber	A device designed to limit the shock load on equipment and anchor points generated by a fall to 6kN – also thereby minimising the impact load absorbed by the body of the faller. It may do this by deforming under a shock load.
etrier	System of loops to provide foot and hand purchase using rope or tape mimicking a rope ladder.
existing place of work	An existing building or permanent structure including its means of access or egress from which there is no risk of a fall occurring. It does not require the use or addition of any work equipment to prevent a fall.
exposure	**(a)** a subjective measure of the insecurity induced by the effect of height and/or an area of expanse beneath the operator/rescuer. **(b)** cooling of the body resulting from an inability of the body's metabolism to generate heat as rapidly as the environment is removing it, often leading to Hypothermia.
factor of safety	The figure by which the breaking strength of new rope is divided to determine its safe working load.
fail safe	A term used to describe either a device that will auto-lock when used in accordance with the manufacturers instructions, or a system with sufficient redundancy that should any one item fail, there is adequate back-up to prevent an accident.
failure load; breaking load	Minimum breaking load of an item of equipment when it is new, previously called breaking strain.
fall arrest	Technique using PPE to safely arrest a fall in the event of loss of controlled contact with the working surface.
fall factor	A measure of the maximum force of a fall expressed as a number – derived from the height or distance of the fall divided by the length of rope in the belay or fall arrest system. The higher the figure the more serious the effects of the fall.
hazard zone	An area inside the field of operations within which the degree of risk from potential hazards including falls or falling objects is sufficient to warrant the application of special control measures.
hawser-laid	Rope made of three strands laid up in the form of a helix in the opposite direction to the lay of the strands.
hitch	A simple fastening of a rope to some object by passing the rope round the object and crossing one part over the other.

impact force	The force generated by a fall – depends principally on the fall factor, the weight of the faller or load, the elasticity of the components that link the faller or load to the anchor (primarily the rope) and the amount of friction in the system.
karabiner	Type of connector, formed as a complete loop, with a spring loaded entry gate often lockable in the closed position by a screwed ring (when it is known as a 'screwgate karabiner') or automatic locking device.
kernmantel rope	Textile rope consisting of a core enclosed by a sheath. The core is usually the main load bearing element and typically consists of parallel elements which have been drawn and turned together in single or several layers, or of braided elements. The sheath is generally braided and protects the core, for example from external abrasion and ultra violet degradation.
knot	The interlacement of cordage in a specific pattern for the purpose of stopping ends, joining ends, forming loops, securing equipment, etc. A knot may be formed with a number of loops, hitches or turns involving any part of a rope or ropes. For the purposes of this manual, the term knot is also deemed to include various bends, lashings and hitches.
laid	A descriptive term to indicate the style of makeup of the rope (see hawser-laid).
lay	The pitch of one complete turn of a strand measured in a straight line parallel to the axis of the rope.
lead climbing	Technique for reaching a higher point during which the climber is protected by ropes, running belays, and a person (known as a belayer) operating a fall arrest device.
life lining or belaying	Method of providing a safety rope to a person operating in a hazard area where a fall or slip is likely. The rope is controlled by a rope control device, operated by the belayer.
lifting equipment	Work equipment for lifting or lowering loads, including attachments used for anchoring, fixing or supporting, e.g. chain or rope sling or similar, ring, link, hook, plate-clamp, shackle, swivel, eyebolt, webbing.
line	Traditional term for cordage cut to a specific length for a particular purpose. Used to differentiate between a full-length rope as originally manufactured (traditionally in imperial measure 120 fathoms, or 720 feet, which equates to 219 metres) and lengths cut from it.

load	Any item that is being lifted, lowered or supported. Under LOLER the term load includes any person, when it is then referred to as a 'liveload'.
low stretch rope	Textile rope with lower elongation and, therefore, less energy absorbing characteristics than dynamic rope.
maillon rapide; screwlink	Screwlink type of connector formed as an open loop, which is closed by a threaded sleeve rather than a hinged gate (see *karabiner*), thus capable of sustaining loads applied in more than two directions. Used where a strong, secure fastening is required that need not be opened or closed quickly. It should be noted that 'maillon rapide' is a trade name, which has come into common use to describe this type of connector.
mousing	An object secured across the opening of a hook to prevent the fastening secured to the hook from unhooking.
natural anchor	A solid object occurring naturally such as a boulder or tree. Must be at least as strong as the rope tied to it unless the load is shared over a number of anchors.
passive rope	Rope which is directly attached to an anchor and which is not moving, such as a rope being used to descend with descent controlled directly by a rescuer.
pay out	To ease out or slacken a rope.
proof load	Test load applied to verify that an item of equipment will not exhibit permanent deformation under that load, at that particular time. This result can then be theoretically related to the performance of the test piece under its expected conditions in service.
prusiking	A method of climbing a fixed rope by means of rope gripping devices such as knots (i.e. prusik knot) or mechanical ascenders.
redundancy	Spare capacity built into the system to ensure that a sufficient degree of safety remains in the event of a partial system failure.
reeve, rove	To thread a rope through a pulley block.
rope	Cordage formed by laying three or more strands together to form a helix round a central axis or by braiding strands around a central core.

rope access	Technique using ropes, normally incorporating two separately secured systems, one as a means of access and the other as a safety back-up, used with a harness in combination with other devices, for getting to and from the place of work and for work positioning.
rope control device	A mechanical device, generally relying on friction, which provides control over the movement of rope or any attached load. Generic name for ascenders, descenders and back-up devices.
rope dog; dogging the tails	Consists of 2 one metre tails of rope at one end and a sewn "thimble" at the other. When laced onto a working rope, it is a method of attaching a hauling system while applying minimum damage. It works on a similar principle to a spliced rope.
rope protection	Protection for rope or other equipment where it passes over or rests on any edge. May also be referred to as edge protection.
running belay	A belay through which a rope is threaded and through which it can move freely.
running end	The free end of the rope.
running part	The moving part of a rope which is loose and is used to hoist or lower.
'safe'	A term to be used by anyone during a training or operational incident when they have reached a position of safety and are secure.
safe working load (SWL)	Designated maximum working load of an item of equipment under particular, specified conditions. See also working load limit (WLL).
safety rope; secondary rope; back-up rope	A rope which is under the control of a competent person and connected via a rope control device to an anchor point in such a way that it will protect a worker against a fall in the event of a slip or a failure of the primary working rope or system.
screwlink; (maillon rapide)	Type of connector formed as an open loop, which is closed by a threaded sleeve rather than a hinged gate (see karabiner), thus capable of sustaining loads applied in more than two directions. Used where a strong, secure fastening is required that need not be opened or closed quickly. It should be noted that 'maillon rapide' is a trade name, which has come into common use to describe this type of connector.
seizing	Binding used to fasten two ropes or parts of one rope to prevent them moving in relation to each other.

shock absorber	See 'energy absorber'.
shock load	The additional load imposed on equipment and anchor points when a fall or movement is stopped suddenly.
splicing	A method of joining two ropes together, or of making an eye in the end of a rope, by unlaying the strands for a short distance and then interlocking the strands of the two parts into one another.
stance	A position where a rope operator can stand balanced on his/her feet with both hands free to work.
standing part	The part of the bight of a rope that is nearest the eye, bend or hitch, as opposed to the end.
static rope	Old term for rope with lower elongation characteristics than dynamic rope, superseded by the term 'low stretch rope'. Now only applies to ropes with negligible stretch, such as wire or Kevlar, which show little extension at failure and hence have little or no ability to absorb shock loads.
tensile strength	The point at which a material no longer has resistance to breakage.
traversing	Broadly horizontal progression, normally in suspension, using aid climbing techniques and/or pulley systems on transverse ropes or cables.
whipping	Binding around the end of a rope to prevent the strands from unlaying (unravelling).
work positioning	A system of work in which the firefighter's weight is supported to allow the firefighter to carry out necessary work by using PPE in tension in such a way as to prevent a fall.
work restraint	Technique using PPE to prevent a firefighter reaching a point where the potential of a fall likely to cause personal injury exists.
working area	Zone outside the 'Hazard Area' where rope operations such as operating pulley systems should be carried out.
working rope	Primary rope used for work positioning or restraint – including for descending and ascending.
working load limit (WLL)	Maximum load that can be lifted by an item of equipment under conditions specified by the manufacturer.

Appendix A – Work at Height Flowchart

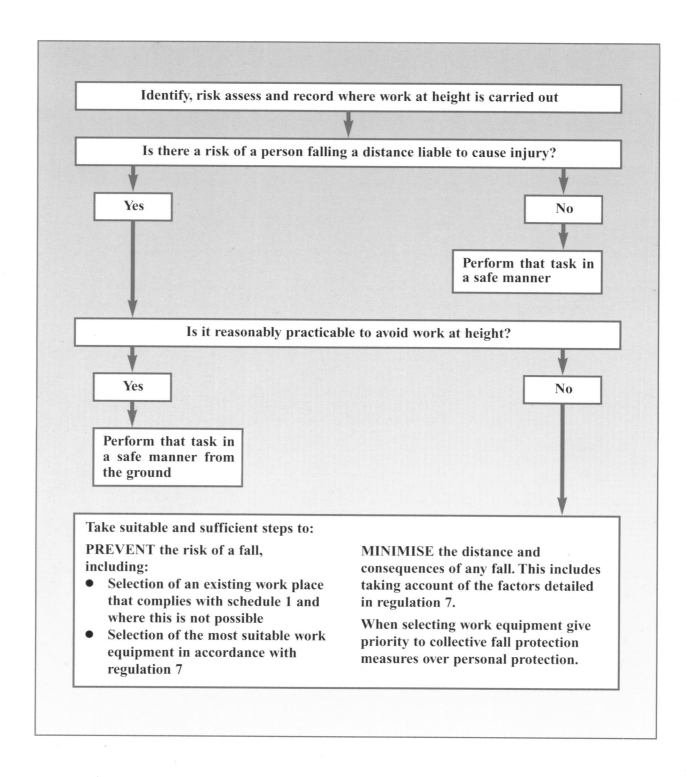

Identify, risk assess and record where work at height is carried out

Is there a risk of a person falling a distance liable to cause injury?

Yes

No

Perform that task in a safe manner

Is it reasonably practicable to avoid work at height?

Yes

No

Perform that task in a safe manner from the ground

Take suitable and sufficient steps to:

PREVENT the risk of a fall, including:
- Selection of an existing work place that complies with schedule 1 and where this is not possible
- Selection of the most suitable work equipment in accordance with regulation 7

MINIMISE the distance and consequences of any fall. This includes taking account of the factors detailed in regulation 7.

When selecting work equipment give priority to collective fall protection measures over personal protection.